The Daily Telegraph

TAX GUIDE 2007

PREPARED BY DAVID B. GENDERS, F.C.A.

ROBINSON
London

Constable & Robinson Ltd
3 The Lanchesters
162 Fulham Palace Road
London W6 9ER
www.constablerobinson.com

First published as *The Daily Telegraph Guide to Income Tax 1974*

31st edition, completely revised, published by Robinson,
an imprint of Constable & Robinson, 2007

ACKNOWLEDGEMENT
The HM Revenue & Customs forms reproduced in this
book are Crown copyright and are reproduced with
the permission of Her Majesty's Stationary Office.

A copy of the British Library Cataloguing in Publication
Data is available from the British Library

ISBN: 978–1–84529–587–5

Printed and bound in the EU

1 3 5 7 9 10 8 6 4 2

CONTENTS

Cash accounting. Annual accounting. Penalties, surcharges and interest. Appeals. Complaints.

About the author

David Genders has been writing *The Daily Telegraph Tax Guide* since 1982. A partner of Sayers Butterworth LLP, Chartered Accountants in London, he joined the firm in 1965 as an apprentice before qualifying as a chartered accountant in 1970. He has since specialized in taxation, focusing on personal tax. Appointed partner in 1977, and senior partner in 2000, David brings a whole career of expertise and experience to the *Tax Guide*.

Away from tax affairs, David enjoys golf, gardening and walking, and harbours an ambition to drive a steam train.

INTRODUCTION

We all want a better education for our children, an improved National Health Service, a more efficient and reliable transport system, less congestion on the roads and to feel safer and more secure in our homes and when we walk the streets. So who has to foot the bill for all these services? The Government, of course. And how does the Government raise the revenues to meet this expenditure? Mainly by taxing income, wealth, production and imports as well as collecting Social contributions from us. Any deficit from one year to the next is funded by borrowing.

The taxes covered in the *Guide* are:

- Income Tax – what we pay annually on our earnings and income from savings.

- Capital Gains Tax – paid only when we realize profits on sales of our assets.

- Inheritance Tax – chargeable on some lifetime gifts of capital and on the value of our Estates on death.

- Value Added Tax – included in the price of many goods and services we buy, mainly at the standard rate of 17.5%.

- National Insurance and Social Security – the contributions we have to pay based on our earnings or business profits and the various benefits, including the State Pension, we receive in return.

- Tax Credits – whether you are eligible and how to work out what you can claim.

For many people tax is both confusing and complicated. This book aims to:

- explain the basics of the taxes covered for the average taxpayer as straightforwardly as possible;

- help the reader have a better understanding of their tax affairs and, therefore, be able to take control;

- make staying within the law as easy as possible; and

- help cut tax bills with pointers to saving on tax.

This edition of the *Tax Guide* is primarily intended to cover the Self-Assessment tax year from 6 April 2006 to 5 April 2007 and is being published at about the time you should be receiving a Tax Return for this year. I hope you benefit from the read.

1 YOU AND HMRC

Ask any taxpayer the question 'Would you like to pay less tax?' and I imagine that, almost without exception, the answer would be 'Yes'.

By the time you have finished reading this book I would like to think that you will have come across at least one way of saving tax, maybe:

- another allowance or relief you can claim;
- an expense that could be included in your business accounts; or
- a more tax-efficient structuring of your cash deposits and investments.

But, first of all, you should have an understanding of the workings of the various HMRC departments responsible for the day-to-day running of our tax system.

HM Revenue & Customs (HMRC) was formally launched back in 2005 following the merger of the former departments of the Inland Revenue and HM Customs & Excise.

The Board of HMRC has overall authority for administering the fiscal legislation enacted by Government. Although there are a large number of specialist departments within HMRC, it is likely that your only contact with HMRC will be through the staff at your Tax Office and the Collector of Taxes.

Tax Offices

Each tax office throughout the country is headed up by a Senior Officer with a full support staff. The tax affairs of employees and pensioners are looked after by the tax office that deals with the Pay-As-You-Earn affairs of their employer or pension fund. If you are self-employed you will find that the tax office responsible for your tax affairs is often local to your business address.

Currently there are the following types of tax office:

Service Office

It is your Service Office which:

- sends you a Tax Return to complete each year;
- processes your Return when you send it back;
- corrects any obvious or simple errors which you have made and sends you a notice detailing the amendments; and
- initially chases you up if you are late sending in your Return.

Service Offices are also responsible for:

- looking after all the day-to-day tax matters of the vast majority of taxpayers whose income is taxed under Pay-As-You-Earn and do not come within the system of Self-Assessment; and
- processing the business accounts of self-employed taxpayers.

As long as you comply with all your tax obligations and in a timely manner, your only involvement with HMRC will be confined to your Service Office.

Compliance Office

Often situated in the same office block as a Service Office each Compliance Office is responsible for:

- providing technical assistance to the local Service Office;
- investigating the Tax Returns and business accounts of those taxpayers selected for further attention; and
- beginning enforcement and recovery action of late Tax Returns or payments.

Complex Personal Returns (CPR)

The tax affairs of wealthy taxpayers with complex Tax Returns are dealt with by one of HMRC's CPR teams. Taxpayers so affected should always receive a letter telling them what is happening and advising them of the name and telephone number of their 'personal case owner'.

Tax Enquiry Centre

The address and telephone number of your nearest Tax Enquiry Centre are in your local telephone book under HMRC. The functions of such offices are to:

- help with enquiries and provide assistance personally or over the telephone;

- accept payments of tax from taxpayers who prefer to pay locally; and

- supply forms and leaflets.

A list of the remaining helpful booklets on different aspects of our tax system published by HMRC (Revenue) is set out in Appendix 1 at the end of the book. Many of the leaflets have now been withdrawn and replaced by online guidance.

The Collector of Taxes

The main tasks of HMRC Accounts Offices are to:

- bank payments of tax and National Insurance Contributions; and

- keep up-to-date accurate payments records.

If you need to telephone, write to or visit any of these offices please always give your name and reference number. You can find the address and telephone number on forms and letters that have been sent to you.

Business by telephone

If your tax affairs are handled by a Tax District which is part of a Contact Centre the following services are available to you by telephone:

- personal information such as changes of address or in your personal circumstances;

- employment details;

- claims to personal allowances;

- claims for either tax relief on flat-rate expenses (see Appendix 2 at the end of the book) or certain professional subscriptions to be included in the PAYE coding for the current year;

- employee benefits such as a company car, fuel for private motoring and medical insurance which affect your PAYE coding;

- other information such as the receipt of a State Pension;

- making certain amendments to your Self-Assessment Return; and

- dealing with tax repayments due to you.

In most cases nothing more will be needed from you, although the call may lead to further action by HMRC (for example, sending out a revised PAYE Coding Notice). Where your business cannot be completely dealt with by telephone, the HMRC officer will arrange to send you any necessary forms or follow-up material.

When you telephone do not be put off by any steps taken to establish your identity. Any such checks are for the purpose of safeguarding the privacy of your tax affairs.

Dealing with your Tax Office

On any straightforward matter, which does not come within the 'business by telephone' services, if you want a quick answer it is better to telephone your Tax Office. You will be put through to one of the Tax Inspector's assistants who should be able to help you with an enquiry about any of the following:

- general questions about Income Tax and Capital Gains Tax;

- specific questions affecting your own tax liability;

- help with completing Tax Returns and other HMRC forms; and

- requests for leaflets, forms and other HMRC information.

On more involved aspects of your tax affairs I recommend you put these in writing to your Tax Office. Occasionally you may want to make a visit to your Tax Office for a detailed discussion on a particular matter of your tax affairs. Where this is a long way from your home or place of work you can always visit a local HMRC office or your nearest Tax Enquiry Centre.

Whenever you telephone or write always remember to quote your reference number which is:

- your employer's PAYE reference; or

- your National Insurance Number; or

- if you are self-employed or pay tax at the higher rate, your Self-Assessment Unique Taxpayer Reference (UTR). This is a 10-digit number.

Enquiries

Once your Return has been processed by your Tax Office, it will undergo a comprehensive programme of checks. Any obvious errors, for example in your arithmetic, will be corrected and no further enquiries will probably be made. But enquiries will be started by your Tax Office if:

- something requires fuller explanation;
- there is a risk your Return may be incorrect; or
- your Return is selected for enquiry at random.

Normally HMRC have 12 months from the filing date for your Return in which to tell you that it will be the subject of enquiries. A longer period of time is allowed where you are late sending in your Return.

Beth Adams completes her Tax Return for the year to 5 April 2007 on 14 August of that year and immediately posts it to her Tax Office. The latest filing date for her 2006/07 Return is 31 January 2008. Therefore, her Tax Office has until 31 January 2009 in which to raise any enquiries.

But Beth's husband, Simon, is slow about filling in his Return and only submits it on 6 February 2008. His Tax Office can raise enquiries at any time up to 30 April 2009.

Your Return will normally become final if your Tax Office has not raised any enquiries within the permitted time period. HMRC can only raise enquiries at a later date if they discover an error which they could not reasonably have been expected to be aware of from the information provided in, or with, your Return.

At the end of an enquiry into your Return HMRC will issue a closure notice which will include the making of any necessary adjustments to your Self-Assessment. You have 30 days in which to appeal against such amendments.

Any enquiries by your Tax Office should be conducted in accordance with the specific code of practice laid down by HMRC. If your Tax Return ever becomes the subject of an enquiry this may well be a time when you should be represented by a professional tax adviser.

Determinations

Not surprisingly HMRC has special powers to deal with taxpayers who are sent a Return but fail to complete it and submit it by the filing date. In such cases an offending taxpayer can expect HMRC to make a determination of his or her income and capital gains chargeable to tax to the best of their knowledge and belief. The actual amount of tax is based on estimates of:

- the taxpayer's allowances and reliefs; and

- tax deducted at source on earnings and savings income.

Any determination can be subsequently superseded by a Self-Assessment by the taxpayer or HMRC based on information provided by the taxpayer.

Assessments and appeals

In cases of fraud or neglect your Inspector of Taxes can raise an assessment to collect tax which should have been paid on a Self-Assessment.

You do, of course, have a right of appeal against:

- an assessment raised by your Tax Inspector; or

- an amendment to your Return following an enquiry.

The procedure for resolving your appeal starts with a hearing before the General or Special Tax Commissioners. It can then move on to the courts and ultimately to the House of Lords.

Prosecutions

An important role of HMRC is to deter fraud. They will prosecute in serious cases in all areas of the tax system. Cases selected for prosecution involve a wide range of offences. However, a case is more likely to be considered for prosecution if it contains features such as:

- falsification of documents;

- lying during an investigation;

- conspiracy; or

- discovery of false documents made during an earlier investigation.

The Service Commitment

The standards of customer service to which HMRC is dedicated are laid down in its Service Commitment, the text of which is as follows:

HMRC is committed to serving your needs well by

- *acting fairly and impartially*

  we

  — treat your affairs in strict confidence, within the law

  — want you to pay or receive only the right amount due

- *communicating effectively with you*

  we aim to provide

  — clear and simple forms and guidance

  — accurate and complete information in a helpful and appropriate way

- *providing good quality service*

  we aim to

  — handle your affairs promptly and accurately

  — be accessible in ways that are convenient to you

  — keep your costs to the minimum necessary

  — take reasonable steps to meet special needs

  — be courteous and professional

- *taking responsibility for our service*

  — we publish annually our customer-service aims and achievements

  — if you wish to comment, or make a complaint, we want to hear from you so we can improve our service. We advise you how to do this

- *providing a better service if you help us by*
  - — keeping accurate and up-to-date records
  - — letting us know if your personal/business circumstances change
  - — giving us correct and complete information when we ask for it
  - — paying on time what you should pay

Complaints

Any complaint should, first of all, be made to the Tax Office with which you are dealing. Address your letter to the Officer in Charge, describe the complaint (slow service, constant mistakes) and the remedy you want (an apology, compensation).

Most complaints about HMRC's handling of people's tax affairs are satisfactorily settled by their Tax Office. Where taxpayers are not satisfied with the response from their office, they can complain to:

- senior local management;
- HMRC's Head Office;
- a Member of Parliament; or
- the Parliamentary Commission for Administration.

Taxpayers who are still dissatisfied can put their case to the HMRC Adjudicator, who will consider complaints about the way in which HMRC:

- has handled someone's tax affairs – for example, complaints about excessive delay, errors, discourtesy; or
- has exercised discretion.

The Adjudicator will review all the facts and try to reach a decision as soon as possible. HMRC normally accepts this decision except where there are exceptional circumstances. The Board of HMRC receives an annual report from the Adjudicator which serves as a useful mechanism in identifying problem areas and required changes.

Changes in legislation

Every year in March or early April the Chancellor of the Exchequer makes his annual Budget Statement. This is preceded by a Pre-Budget Report in the previous November or December. Not only does he use these occasions to report on the nation's finances, but they are the times when he tells us about:

- tax rates and allowances for the following year; and

- new or amending legislation to our tax laws.

Resulting legislative changes are published in a Finance Bill. Its various clauses are debated by Parliament and occasionally amended. Subsequently, the Bill is passed by both Houses of Parliament before receiving Royal Assent. It is then published as a Finance Act.

When the law is either unclear or ambiguous HMRC will issue a Statement of Practice indicating how they intend to interpret it. There are also times when HMRC does not seek to go by the strict letter of the law. These are gathered together and published as a list of Extra-Statutory Concessions.

2   TAX RATES AND ALLOWANCES

For most of us our annual tax bill is simply dependent on:

*   tax bands and rates; and

*   the allowances and credits we can claim.

Income Tax rates

Under our tax system, the tax (or fiscal) year runs from each 6 April to the following 5 April.

The rates of tax for 2006/07 are:

Band of Taxable Income	Rate of Tax	Tax on Band	Cumulative Tax
£	%	£	£
0–2,150	10	215.00	215.00
2,151–33,300	22	6,853.00	7,068.00
over 33,300	40		

The rate of 10% is known as the starting rate. The basic rate is 22% and tax at 40% is referred to as the higher rate.

Savings income, apart from dividends, is generally taxed at:

*   20% on income above the £2,150 starting rate limit but below the basic rate limit of £33,300; and

*   40% above the basic rate limit.

Income from UK dividends is taxed at:

*   10% on dividend income within the basic rate limit of £33,300; and

*   32.5% above the basic rate limit.

Allowances

You can reduce the income on which you pay tax by claiming any of the allowances to which you are entitled.

The rates of the various tax allowances for 2006/07 are:

	£
Personal	
aged under 65	5,035
aged 65–74	7,280
aged 75 and over	7,420
Married Couples	
born before 6 April 1935	
and aged less than 75	*6,065
aged 75 and over	*6,135
minimum amount	*2,350
Relief for Blind person (each)	1,660

* Indicates allowances where tax relief is restricted to 10%

Allowances on which tax relief is unrestricted are deducted from total income in working out the amount of Income Tax you pay each year. Tax relief for the other allowances, highlighted by an asterisk in the above table, is given as a deduction from tax payable.

Indexation

Unless Parliament decides otherwise most allowances and the tax rate bands are linked to annual inflation increases. This upward movement is in line with the increase in the Retail Prices Index (RPI) during the year to the end of September prior to the tax year and applies to:

- the bands of income taxable at the starting and basic rates;
- the personal allowances;
- the married couple's allowances;
- blind person's relief; and
- the income limit for age allowances.

Personal allowance

Every man, woman or child, single or married, resident in the UK can claim the personal allowance. This is set against total income on which Income Tax is payable such as:

- a wage, salary or business profits;

- an occupational and/or a State Pension; and

- income from investments.

During 2006/07, Richard West, a married man in his early 40s, earned £26,000 from his job. His tax liability for the year is £4,354.30, worked out as follows:

	£
Salary	26,000
Less: Personal allowance	5,035
Taxable income	20,965
Income Tax payable	
£2,150 @ 10%	215.00
£18,815 @ 22%	4,139.30
	£4,354.30

As the table on the previous page shows, the amount of your annual personal allowance depends on your age. A pensioner, aged 65 years or over for part or all of the tax year, is eligible for the personal age allowance. There is an enhanced personal age allowance for elderly taxpayers who are over 74 years old during part or all of a tax year.

Married couple's allowance

A married couple living together can benefit from the married couple's allowance so long as one spouse was at least 65 years old on 5 April 2000.

For couples married before 5 December 2005 it is the husband who should make the claim. Thereafter the allowance is given to the spouse with the higher income. This option is also available, by election, to couples married up to 4 December 2005. The amount of this allowance is determined by the age of the elder spouse.

Eric Black was 78 years old in 2006/07. His younger wife, Myra, celebrated her 63rd birthday the same year. They are entitled to allowances of £13,555 and £5,035 as follows:

	Eric	Myra
	£	£
Personal age/personal	7,420	5,035
Married couple's	6,135	—
Total allowances	£13,555	£5,035

Another elderly couple, Donald and Sylvia Temple, both enjoyed their 72nd birthdays in the summer of 2006. Their total allowances for 2006/07 are £13,345 and £7,280 as follows:

	Donald	Sylvia
	£	£
Personal age	7,280	7,280
Married couple's	6,065	—
Total allowances	£13,345	£7,280

The amount of the married couple's allowance in the year of marriage depends upon the time in the year that the wedding takes place. The allowance is reduced by one-twelfth for every complete month from 6 April up to the day of the marriage.

Percy Hughes, aged 72, married his wife, Barbara, aged 67, on 11 November 2006. He receives an allowance of £2,527 for 2006/07 worked out as follows:

	£
Married couple's allowance	6,065
Less: Reduction	
$^7/_{12}$ x £6,065	3,538
2006/07 Allowance	£2,527

There is no reduction in the married couple's allowance for a year when:

- couples separate;

- couples divorce; or

- one spouse dies.

A widow is entitled to any unused part of the married couple's allowance for the year in which she loses her husband.

A wife does not need her husband's consent to claim one half of the minimum amount of the married couple's allowance, £1,175 for 2006/07. Alternatively, a married couple can jointly elect for the wife to receive the full minimum amount of the allowance, £2,350 for 2006/07. Such an election:

- must be made using HMRC Form 18;

- must normally be made before the start of the tax year for which it is to apply (except in the year of marriage when the newly-weds can submit immediately a notice dealing with the reduced married couple's allowance for that year); and

- once made carries on from year to year until changed by the couple.

Without the above election the husband is entitled to the full married couple's allowance. But, if he is on a low income and cannot make full use of this allowance, he can transfer any excess allowance to his wife by completing Form 575.

Civil partners

From 5 December 2005 it has been possible for same-sex couples to have legal recognition of their relationship by forming a Civil Partnership. This is an equality measure for same-sex couples who are unable to marry.

Since Civil Partnership is a parallel status to marriage, the tax system has been adapted so that the various rules dealing with the taxation of married couples now also apply to civil partners.

Long standing partners, Rex Gardner and Gerald Sullivan, entered into a civil partnership on 9 January 2006. They are both in their late 70's. Gerald, who has the higher income, can claim the married couple's allowance of £6,135 for 2006/07.

Age allowances – income limit

The purpose of the personal age and married couples allowances is to assist those pensioners on low and modest incomes. It follows, therefore, that these allowances are restricted when total income, after permitted reliefs and deductions, exceeds a specified limit – £20,100 for 2006/07. The reduction is £1 for each £2 by which total income is more than the annual stated limit. However:

- the reduced personal allowance cannot come to less than £5,035; and

- there is a minimum amount of £2,350 for the married couple's allowance.

The personal age allowance decreases first. When it comes to working out any restriction to the married couple's allowance, this calculation is based solely on the husband's income or the spouse/civil partner with the higher income, as the case may be. It is unaffected by the wife's income or that of the other civil partner no matter how much this is.

It follows that any benefit of the higher personal age allowance is lost when income exceeds £24,590 for a taxpayer aged 65–74 and £24,870 for a pensioner over age 74.

The upper income limits for the claimant beyond which the married couple's allowance reduces to the minimum amount for 2006/07 are:

	Wife's/Partner's Age	
Claimant's Age	*65–74	Over 74
	£	£
Under 65	27,530	27,670
*65–74	32,020	32,160
Over 74	32,440	32,440

* Born before 6 April 1935

An elderly couple, Andrew Dawson, aged 74, and his wife Monica, aged 77, whose income amounted to £25,000 and £21,000 respectively during 2006/07 paid Income Tax of £3,481.30 and £2,804.60 respectively, worked out as follows:

	Andrew	Monica
	£	£
Income		
State Pensions	4,381	2,626
Pensions from former employers	17,619	17,174
Building Society Interest	3,000	1,200
	25,000	21,000
Less: Personal allowance	5,035	6,970
Taxable Income	£19,965	£14,030
Income Tax payable		
£2,150 @ 10%	215.00	215.00
£14,815/£10,680 @ 22%	3,259.30	2,349.60
£3,000/£1,200 @ 20%	600.00	240.00
	4,074.30	2,804.60
Less: Relief for married couple's allowance – £5,930 @ 10%	593.00	—
	£3,481.30	£2,804.60

Andrew does not get any benefit from the personal age allowance as his income is more than £24,590. Monica's personal age allowance of £7,420 is reduced by £450 = 0.5 x £900 (£21,000 – income limit of £20,100).

The married couple's allowance of £6,135 is initially restricted by £2,450 = 0.5 x (£25,000 – £20,100). But Andrew's loss of personal allowance of £2,245 limits the loss of relief to £205 (from £6,135 to £5,930).

Blind person's relief

This relief is given to a registered blind person. Where both husband and wife or both civil partners are blind each of them can claim the relief. If either of them is on a low income and unable to use up his or her relief, any unused part can be transferred to the other even if he or she is not blind.

When a taxpayer first becomes entitled to this special relief, by being registered blind, the relief will also be given for the previous tax year if, at the time, the individual had received the necessary proof of blindness needed to qualify for registration. This concession prevents individuals losing out as a result of any delays in the registration process.

3 TAX CREDITS

To qualify for Tax Credits you must be:

- aged 16 or over; and

- usually living in the United Kingdom.

Married couples, couples living together as partners and civil partners must submit a single joint application.

Both Tax Credits are dependent on the incomes of the claimants.

Child Tax Credit

Child Tax Credit (CTC) is:

- available to individuals responsible for at least one child or qualifying young person; and

- paid by direct transfer to the bank account of the person (usually the mother) mainly responsible for the care of the child or children.

A child is a person under 16 years old or in the case of a 16-year-old teenager, until 1 September next after their 16th birthday. A qualifying young person is someone who is:

- no longer a child;

- under 20 years old; and

- in full-time education.

CTC is made up of the following elements:

Rates for 2006/07	Annual	Weekly
	£	£
Family element	545.00	10.45
Family element, baby addition (first year only)	545.00	10.45
Child element (each child)	1,765.00	33.95
Disability element	2,350.00	45.20
Severe disability element	945.00	18.20

Working Tax Credit

The Working Tax Credit (WTC) can be claimed by individuals who are:

- employed or self-employed;

- over age 24, without children, and usually work for at least 30 hours a week; or

- usually undertake paid work for at least 16 hours a week, are aged 16 and over and either responsible for at least one child or disabled.

WTC is paid directly to both employees and the self-employed by HMRC.

Recipients of WTC may also qualify for assistance with the costs of childcare. In such circumstances the childcare element of WTC is paid with entitlement to CTC, to the person responsible for the care of the child or children.

WTC comprises the following elements:

Rates for 2006/07	Annual	Weekly
	£	£
Basic entitlement	1,665.00	32.00
Additional couples, and lone parent, element	1,640.00	31.50
30 hour element	680.00	13.10
Disability element	2,225.00	42.80
Severe disability element	945.00	18.20
50 plus return to work payment, for 16–29 hours	1,140.00	21.90
50 plus return to work payment, for 30+ hours	1,705.00	32.80
Childcare element		
– maximum eligible cost		300.00
– maximum eligible cost for one child		175.00
Percentage of eligible cost covered		80%

Tapering

Tax Credits taper away at a rate of 37% for each £1 of family income over a threshold of £5,220 (£14,155 where no WTC is claimed). The order of reduction is:

- Working Tax Credit;
- childcare element; and
- child elements of Child Tax Credit.

The family element and baby addition of CTC are tapered at a different rate by reference to:

- a second threshold of £50,000; and
- a different withdrawal rate of 1 in 15.

Sharon and Ken Bailey have three children, two sons aged 8 and 6 and a baby daughter born on 21 November 2006.

Ken works full time and earns a salary of £18,000. Sharon stays at home to look after the children. Before tapering their total entitlement to Tax Credits for 2006/07 is:

	£	£
Working Tax Credit		
Basic entitlement	1,665.00	
Additional couples element	1,640.00	
30 hour element	680.00	
	———	3,985.00
Child Tax Credit		
Family element	545.00	
Baby addition	545.00	
Child element (3)	5,295.00	
	———	6,385.00

The effect of tapering is to reduce entitlement by £4,728.60 (being 37% × £18,000 − £5,220). As a result Ken receives no WTC and the CTC paid to Sharon is reduced by £743.60 to £5,641.40.

Alison Baldwin is a single parent. She looks after her two daughters aged 4 and 2. She pays £260 per week for childcare costs. Alison is a successful businesswoman earning a salary of £35,000 per annum. Her Tax Credits for the 2006/07 tax year work out at £7,858 as follows:

	£	£
Working Tax Credit		
Basic entitlement	1,665.00	
Lone parent element	1,640.00	
30 hour element	680.00	
Childcare element	*10,816.00	
	————	14,801.00
Child Tax Credit		
Child element (2)	3,530.00	
Family element	545.00	
	————	4,075.00
		18,876.00
Less: Taper 37% × £29,780 (£35,000 – £5,220)		11,018.00
		————
Total Credits		£7,858.00

* £208 per week being 80% of the cost of £260 per week.

Annual Renewal

From around April each year onwards an existing claimant will receive a letter telling him or her how to finalise the award for the year just finished and make a claim for the following year. You have until 31 August in which to provide the information requested. Once your reply has been processed you will receive a notice about your final Tax Credit for that year.

If you have received too much Tax Credit you will be expected to refund the excess. This will usually be done by restricting the award for the following year.

If you have been paid too little Tax Credit you will receive the extra as a single payment.

Changes in Circumstances

Once a claimant has been granted Tax Credits, even for a nil amount, he or she has a duty to advise HMRC within one month of certain stipulated changes in circumstances which are:

- the number of children for which support can be claimed;

- in work status;

- marriage, moving in to live with a partner or entering a civil partnership;

- separation;

- discontinuing payment to a childcare provider for at least four weeks continuously; and/or

- a drop of more than £10 a week in costs of childcare, again for at least four weeks in a row.

There may be other changes in circumstances, such as the birth of a child that should be notified to HMRC particularly to avoid losing out on an award.

Income Disregard

Not only is a claimant's entitlement to tax credits continuously adjusted by alterations in lifestyle circumstances but it is also affected by changes to income in the award period, namely a tax year. Therefore, when a claimant's income drops, a higher award can be immediately requested. Conversely when income increases the amount of the award will come down.

It is, however, provided that a claimant's income for tax credit purposes can increase by as much as £25,000 in a claim year, compared to the previous year, without any reduction in entitlement. This gives more certainty to claimants that their payments will not suddenly be decreased when their income goes up during an award period.

Penalties and Interest

The following penalties can be charged:

Offence	Penalty
Failure to notify a change of circumstances within 3 months.	£300
Failure to provide information or evidence required by HMRC, to include omitting to fill in and return a renewal form on time.	An initial penalty of £300 followed by penalties of up to £60 per day for continuing failure.
Negligent or fraudulent claims.	Up to £3,000

Interest is charged by HMRC at 6.5%, or Bank Base Rate plus 2.5%, where Tax Credits are overpaid, wholly or partly resulting from a claimant's fraud or neglect.

Help and Advice

If you would like help or advice about Tax Credits you can phone the Helpline on 0845 300 3900 (England, Scotland and Wales) or 0845 603 2000 (Northern Ireland). You may also be able to get assistance from a local advice service such as a Citizens' Advice Bureau.

4 INTEREST PAYMENTS AND OTHER OUTGOINGS

The opportunities for claiming tax relief on interest paid on borrowings are few and far between. They are for:

- the purchase, in certain circumstances, of life annuities if you are aged 65 or over;

- buying a share in:

  — an employee-controlled company;

  — a close company (i.e. controlled by five or fewer shareholders), or lending capital to it;

  — a partnership, or contributing capital to a partnership, if you are a partner;

- buying plant and machinery for use in your job or partnership so long as the plant and machinery attracts capital allowances for tax purposes (see Chapter 6).

Interest is also allowable for tax purposes on a replacement loan where the interest on existing borrowings qualifies for tax relief.

It is important to understand that the purpose for which a loan is advanced governs whether the interest on it will be eligible for tax relief. How the loan is secured is not relevant.

Apart from interest on a loan to acquire buy-to-let property, the interest on which tax relief is due is deducted from your total income in the year of payment. It cannot be spread over the period of accrual, nor can tax relief be claimed if the interest is not actually paid.

Home annuity loans

Interest on a loan taken out before 9 March 1999 to purchase an annuity (an investment providing a fixed or increasing annual sum) from an insurance company still attracts tax relief at 23% provided:

- the borrower was at least 65 years old at the time the annuity was purchased;

- not less than 90% of the loan on which the interest is payable went towards buying an annuity for life; or

- security for the loan is the borrower's main residence.

The maximum loan on which tax relief is allowed is £30,000. Where a loan exceeds this limit tax relief is given on the proportion of the total interest payable equivalent to the £30,000 limit. Income Tax at the special rate of 23% will be deducted at source by the insurance company in working out the regular payments to be made by the borrower.

Buy-to-let property

Interest on a loan taken out to buy, improve or alter a property which you let out is tax deductible. The interest paid each year is set against the rental income from the property and any other properties which you are renting out as part of your income from property business. If the interest paid exceeds the rent less expenses in the same tax year, the excess cannot be set against your other income. The loss can only be carried forward for offset against rental income in future years.

Lionel Foster acquired a buy-to-let flat in 1998 with the assistance of a mortgage of £120,000. His rents less expenses came to £2,500 and £11,000 during 2005/06 and 2006/07 respectively.

	2005/06		2006/07	
	£	£	£
Rents less expenses	2,500		11,000
Less: Loan interest paid	6,000	6,500	
Loss carried forward	£3,500	3,500	
			10,000
2006/07 Net rental income			£1,000

Business loans

Interest on any borrowings by your business can count as a deduction from your business profits for tax purposes. Provided that the borrowed money is used for business purposes it does not matter whether the interest is paid on:

- a loan taken out for some specific purpose; or

- borrowings because your bank account goes overdrawn.

Interest you pay will also qualify for tax relief where you need to borrow to:

- buy an asset, such as a car or a piece of machinery, for use in your business. The tax allowable interest will be restricted by the extent of any private usage; or

- purchase a share in a partnership of which you are about to become a member, or to contribute capital for use in its business.

Perhaps, however, you have business connections with a private company? Interest paid on a loan raised so you can either buy shares in the company, or lend it money for use in its business, is tax deductible. You must either:

- own at least 5% of the company's share capital; or

- hold at least some shares in the company and spend the greater part of your time working in the business.

Employees who need to borrow to buy shares in their company, as part of an employee buy-out, are allowed tax relief on the interest paid on their borrowings.

Gift Aid

Gift Aid is an Income Tax relief for cash gifts, without limit, by individuals to charities. Under Gift Aid a charity can reclaim back from HMRC the basic-rate tax on your cash donation, thereby increasing the value of the gift to the charity. For example, a cash gift of £10 is worth £12.82 to a charity under Gift Aid.

You can:

- give any amount, large or small, regular or one-off;
- pay by cash, cheque, postal order, standing order, direct debit, or by using your credit or debit card.

For your donation to qualify under Gift Aid you must:

- pay at least as much tax in the tax year in which you make your cash gifts as the charities will reclaim on them; and
- make a declaration to the charity that you want your donation to be regarded as made under Gift Aid.

If you pay tax at the top rate of 40% you can claim tax relief on the difference between the higher and basic rates of tax on all your Gift Aid payments.

Norman Walton gave donations totalling £1,560 under Gift Aid in 2006/07. Norman is a higher rate taxpayer so he can reduce his tax bill by £360 as follows:

	£
Grossed-up donations – $£1{,}560 \times \dfrac{100}{78} =$	2,000
Tax relief thereon at 40%	800
Less: Deducted when making donations	440
Reduction in Income Tax payable	£360

You can claim to carry back donations so they are treated as if paid in the previous tax year. For example, donations made after 5 April 2007; and

- before 31 January 2008; or
- the date when you send your 2006/07 Tax Return to your Tax Office (if earlier)

can be carried back to 2006/07 so you get the tax relief in that year rather than in the year of payment.

Self-Assessment Tax Returns include a facility for individuals to give a tax repayment to charity. The main features of this arrangement are:

- you can choose a charity from the list published by HMRC;

- you are under no obligation to donate the whole repayment to charity. You can stipulate how much you want to give; and

- donations made this way can also be under Gift Aid.

If you do not pay tax, Gift Aid is not for you.

Gifts of assets to charities

You can claim relief from Income Tax at your top rate of tax for the full market value of any gifts of shares, securities or land and buildings to charities at the time of the gift. The assets that qualify for this type of tax relief are:

- shares or securities listed on, or dealt in, a recognized Stock Exchange;

- units in an authorized unit trust;

- shares in an open-ended investment company;

- an interest in an offshore fund; and

- land and buildings.

This Income Tax relief is in addition to exemption from Capital Gains Tax on such assets given to charities.

Jennifer Pickard pays tax at the higher rate of 40% on a substantial part of her income. In 2006/07 she decided to give shares in a quoted company valued at £5,000 to a registered charity. The taxable capital gain on the shares would have been £3,000 if she had sold them. Jennifer saves tax of £3,200 as follows:

	£
Reduction in Income Tax (40% x £5,000)	2,000
Capital Gains Tax not payable on the gain (40% x £3,000)	1,200
2006/07 Maximum tax saving	£3,200

Payroll giving

If you are in employment there may be another way that you can make tax-efficient gifts to charity. But, first of all, you need to enquire of your employer whether it participates in such an arrangement through a Charity Arrangement approved by HMRC. If so you can ask your employer to make regular deductions from your salary which, as part of the scheme, will be passed on to the charities of your choice. You will receive full Income Tax relief on such donations. There is no limit to the amount you can contribute this way each year.

5 WORKING IN EMPLOYMENT

Most of us have worked for somebody else at some stage in our lives. The earnings from an employment on which Income Tax is payable are:

- a salary or wage;

- a bonus;

- overtime;

- commission;

- tips or gratuities;

- holiday or sick pay;

- part-time earnings;

- director's salary or fees; and

- benefits-in-kind.

The mechanism for collecting the tax due on earnings from an employment is the Pay-As-You-Earn (PAYE) system. It is the responsibility of employers to deduct Income Tax from the earnings of their employees. The total deductions must be paid over to HMRC every month. The PAYE deducted from an employee's earnings is regarded as a credit against the total tax payable by the employee for that tax year. Each employee's individual allowances and reliefs are taken into account by the employer in working out the amount of tax to deduct from the employee's salary or wage. This is possible because HMRC issues all employers with a code number for each employee.

Code numbers

Every employee's annual PAYE Coding Notice sets out:

- on the first lines, the total tax allowances due; and

- on the left-hand side on the lines below, the amounts taken away from the allowances.

The PAYE system allows for the net allowances to be spread evenly throughout the tax year in working out the deductions for Income Tax so as to avoid any substantial variation to the amount of the regular salary cheque or pay packet.

All things being equal this system should ensure that the right amount of tax is deducted from your earnings each year. However, it can only work properly and effectively if you promptly tell your Tax Office of changes in your personal circumstances that affect any of the entries in your Notice of Coding. For example, most Coding Notices for the 2007/08 tax year, beginning on 6 April 2007, were sent out during the early part of the year. This is before your Tax Office will have received your 2007 Tax Return, stating your income, capital gains, reliefs and allowances for the year to 5 April 2007. It follows, therefore, that the information on which all 2007/08 code numbers have been based is out of date. This is why it is important that you check your code number for 2007/08 and tell your Tax Office if:

- alterations are required to your allowances of reliefs;

- you have started receiving a pension;

- there has been a big change in your income; or

- you have moved home.

Your tax allowances for 2007/08 should be correct as all Income Tax allowances for 2007/08 were announced by the Chancellor in his Pre-Budget Report last December. These are:

		£
Personal		5,225
Age	Personal: age 65–74	7,550
	Married couples: age 65–74	*6,285
	Personal: age 75 and over	7,690
	Married couples: age 75 and over	6,365

* and born before 6 April 1935

For 2007/08 the minimum amount of the married couples allowance is £2,440 and the income limit for age allowance is £20,900.

If the March 2007 Budget contains any other changes affecting your 2007/08 Coding Notice your Tax Office will send you details together with an amended Notice.

Below is an illustration of Simon Black's 2007/08 Notice of Coding.

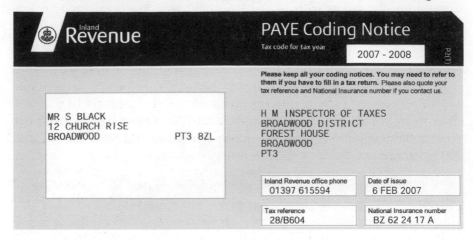

Dear MR S BLACK

Your tax code for the year 6th April 2007 to 5th April 2008 is 38L

You need a tax code so Broadwood Engineers Ltd can work out how much tax to take off the payments they make to you from 6th April 2007. We have worked out your tax code but need you to check that our information about you is correct. The wrong tax code could mean you pay too much, or too little tax. Please keep your coding notices, you may need them if we send you a tax return.

Here is how we worked it out		
your personal allowance		£5225
car benefit	- £1800	
car fuel benefit	- £2160	
medical insurance	- £500	
reduction to collect unpaid tax £83.60	- £380	- £4840
a tax free amount of		£385

If we have got this wrong, or if your circumstances have changed and you think it could affect the tax you pay, please tell us. Our telephone number and address are above. We turn £385 into tax code 38L to send to Broadwood Engineers Ltd. They should use this code with the tables they receive from HMRC to take off the right amount of tax each time they pay you from 6th April 2007. Broadwood Engineers Ltd do not know the details of 38L or how it is worked out – that is confidential between us.

Simon is a married man, with two young children, who does not pay tax at the top rate of 40%. On the first line of the Notice is Simon's personal allowance for 2007/08 of £5,225. The amounts taken away from Simon's allowances are on the lines below. These are:

- The first three deductions are the taxable figures of the benefits-in-kind of a company car, free fuel for private motoring and private medical insurance cover provided to Simon and his family by his employer. The Income Tax payable by Simon on these benefits is, therefore, collected by restricting his allowances by the taxable amount of the benefits.

- The last deduction is for tax of £83.60 underpaid in 2005/06. For a number of reasons the allowances given, or deductions included, in Simon's Notice of Coding may turn out not to be always totally correct. If, as a result, tax is underpaid, this is usually collected in a subsequent year by restricting allowances in the coding. In the illustration a restriction of Simon's 2007/08 allowances by £380 will enable HMRC to collect the underpayment of £83.60 (£380 @ 22%) from him.

The combined effect of these adjustments is to leave Simon with allowances of just £385 to be set against his salary for 2007/08. His code number is 38L. It is not difficult to see that there is a direct link between Simon's allowances and his code number. The suffix letter added to the coding is a way of identifying the category into which a taxpayer falls.

- L is for a code with the basic personal allowance;

- P is for a code with the personal allowance for those aged 65–74;

- V is for a pensioner entitled to both the personal and married couple's allowances for ages 65–74 and who is liable to tax at the basic rate;

- Y is the code if you are due the personal allowance for age 75 and over; and

- T applies in most other cases, for example:

  — if you ask your Tax Office not to use any of the letters listed above; or

  — if there are items in the coding which need to be reviewed.

There are also a number of other codes:

- OT no allowances have been given to you. Tax will be deducted at the starting rate, then the basic rate and finally at the higher rate, depending on your income.

- BR this tells your employer to deduct tax at the basic rate.

- NT means that no tax will be deducted.

- DO tax will be deducted at the top rate of 40%.

- Prefix K – a K code is given to employees whose taxable benefits exceed their personal allowances. The amount of the negative allowances is then added to the pay on which tax is payable. The system of K codes ensures that taxpayers pay all the tax due on their excess benefits evenly throughout the tax year under the PAYE system.

How tax is worked out using your tax code

The coding notice issued to Simon Black for 2007/08 tells him that his tax-free amount for the year is £380. He earns £23,400 per annum in his job.

The deduction for tax is worked out as follows:

	£
Pay from employment	23,400.00
Less: tax-free amount for year	380.00
Tax due on	£23,020.00

	£
Income Tax payable	
£2,150 @ 10%	215.00
£20,870 @ 22%	4,591.40
	£4,806.40

To work out the weekly amounts of pay and tax, divide the pay and tax payable for the year by 52:

Weekly pay is £23,400 ÷ 52 = £450.00

Weekly tax is £4,806.40 ÷ 52 = £92.43

To work out the equivalent monthly amount divide by 12:

Monthly pay is £23,400 ÷ 12 = £1,950.00

Monthly tax is £4,806.40 ÷ 12 = £400.53

Form P60

Shortly after the end of each tax year every employer sends HMRC a Return summarizing:

- the names of all employees;

- their earnings during that tax year; and

- the deductions made for both Income Tax and National Insurance Contributions.

By 31 May following the end of a tax year your employer must give you your Form P60. This is a certificate of your earnings for the past tax year and it also lets you know how much Income Tax and National Insurance Contributions you have paid. On page 36 is an illustration of the Form P60 sent to Simon Black by his employer for 2006/07. This shows:

- the tax deducted from his earnings in the year amounted to £4,580.84 based on a tax code of 19L;

- he incurred National Insurance contributions totalling £1,881.88.

Starting work

If you are starting a job for the first time, or have not already been in work during the tax year, your employer will ask you to fill in a Form P46 and to provide some other information. This will enable your employer to receive a tax code for you from HMRC so that the right deductions for Income Tax can be made from your wage or salary.

Moving jobs

Whenever you change your job your old employer hands you parts 1A, 2 and 3 of a Form P45. On this form are your name and address, the name and address of your past employer, your tax district and reference number, and your code number at the date of leaving. It also includes your cumulative salary and the tax deductions for the tax year up to the date that you leave, and your salary and tax deductions from the last employment unless this information is the same as the cumulative figures. Your ex-employer sends the first part of the Form P45 to his tax district.

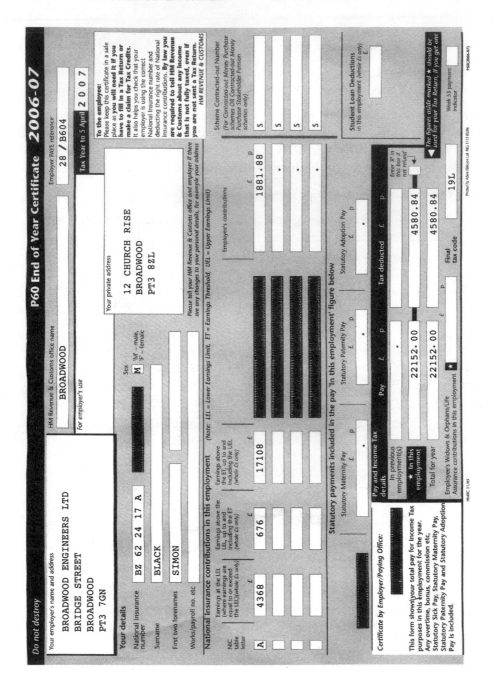

Parts 2 and 3 of the Form P45 must be given to your new employer. He enters your address and the date of starting your latest job before sending part 3 of the form to his own Tax Office. The information from the form allows your current employer to make the correct deductions for

Income Tax and National Insurance from your new salary or wage right from the start of the new job.

You should keep Part 1A of the form for your own records, because it may be helpful when you come to prepare your own Tax Return.

If you do not have a P45 to give to your new employer, you will find that the deductions you incur for Income Tax are equivalent to those of an individual with just a personal allowance. This is known as the 'Emergency' code. Where this happens you should:

- either ask for and complete a Tax Return; or

- send in sufficient information to your new employer's Tax Office so that the correct code number can be issued.

Tax-deductible expenses

The rules allowing you to claim tax relief on expenses connected with your employment are extremely restricted. You are denied tax relief on almost all types of expense which are not ultimately borne by your employer. This is because, as an employee, you have to show that any expenditure is incurred 'wholly, exclusively and necessarily' in performing the duties of your employment. If your employer will not foot the bill for the expenditure involved, then HMRC take the view that it was incurred as a matter of choice rather than of necessity. Nevertheless, some business expenses paid personally are deductible from your income and should be claimed on your Tax Return.

They include:

- annual subscriptions to a professional body;

- business use of your own car and telephone;

- clothing and upkeep of tools – HMRC and the Trade Unions have agreed flat-rate allowances for the upkeep of tools and special clothing in most classes of industry. The current rates are set out in Appendix 2. As an alternative you can claim a deduction for the actual amount spent on these items; and

- payment by directors or employers for work-related insurance cover. Tax relief is also allowed on meeting the cost of uninsured liabilities.

Tax-free expenses

The cost of most expenses you incur in your work is ultimately met by your employer, who either reimburses you on an expense claim or pays for them direct. Tax free for everyone are:

- luncheon vouchers up to 15p per day;

- free or subsidised meals in a staff canteen, providing the facilities can be used by all staff;

- sporting and recreational facilities;

- staff parties, providing the annual cost to the employer is no more then £150 per head;

- awards for long service of at least 20 years. The cost of the articles purchased by the employer must not exceed £50 for each year of service;

- gifts not exceeding £250 in the tax year to an employee from a third party – by reason of his or her employment;

- routine health checks or medical screening;

- eye tests and corrective glasses if your employer is required, by law, to provide eye and eyesight tests for you because of the work you do;

- work-related training expenses including fees, travel, reasonable subsistence and the cost of any books;

- payments made to employees who are required to attend a full-time educational course at a recognized educational establishment. The tax-free limit for an academic year is £15,000 and covers lodging, subsistence and travelling allowances, but excludes any tuition fees payable by the employee to the educational establishment;

- contributions by your employer to your education or training if you are an Individual Learning Account holder. Your employer must make contributions available to all employees on similar terms.

- the cost of out-placement counselling and retraining courses for both full- and part-time employees;

- equipment or facilities provided to disabled people to enable them to carry out their jobs;

- computer equipment loaned to employees before 6 April 2006 providing the cash equivalent of the benefit does not come to more than £500 annually. Any excess over £500 is taxable;

- one mobile telephone per employee for private use. But the exemption continues for multiple telephones provided to employees before 6 April 2006;

- childcare facilities at the workplace or elsewhere (but not on domestic premises);

- employer-supported childcare of up to £55 a week. Employers can either contract with an approved child carer or provide childcare vouchers;

- up to £2 per week paid to you by your employer for working at home as part of your employment contract. You are not required to produce any supporting evidence of the costs you incur;

- personal incidental expenses when you stay away from home overnight on business. The most common expenses covered are newspapers, telephone calls to home and laundry. The tax-free limits, including VAT, are £5 per night for stays anywhere in the UK and £10 per night elsewhere. Where these limits are exceeded the whole payment becomes payable – not the excess;

- bicycle and cycling safety equipment made available to employees mainly to get them between home and work;

- parking facilities for cars, motorcycles or bicycles at or near your place of work;

- a works' bus service;

- the cost of infrequent private transport when you have been working late and either public transport is no longer available or it would be unreasonable to expect you to use it at a late hour. Infrequent late working means working until at least 9.00 pm not more than 60 times in a tax year; and

- mileage allowances where employees use their car, van, motorcycle or pedal cycle on business. The tax-free rates laid down by HMRC for 2006/07 are:

Cars and Vans	
— First 10,000 miles	40p per mile
— Excess	25p per mile
Motorcycles	24p per mile
Bicycles	20p per mile

Employees are taxed on payments made by their employers over and above the rates in the table, but they can claim back on the difference where their employers pay them less than the permitted rate.

Employee travel

The cost of travelling between home and work is not allowable for tax purposes, other than for disabled employees who are given financial help by their employers with home-to-work travel on public transport or by some other means.

However, tax relief is allowed on all your business travel where your journey starts from either home or your permanent workplace. Where the full cost of a journey is not reimbursed by your employer, you can claim tax relief on the excess miles not paid for by your employer.

(a) Site-based workers

These are employees who work at a number of different places for periods of a few weeks or months at a time. Travelling expenses reimbursed to them are tax free providing:

- the worker initially expects the posting not to exceed two years, and the stay must actually last for less than this time;

- there is no requirement for an employee to return to his or her permanent workplace when each site job comes to an end; or

- an employee's work on site may be considered as a single continuous period even if he or she is occasionally moved off-site.

(b) Employees with areas

The geographical area covered by employees such as salesmen is treated as their permanent place of work. The following special rules apply:

- all travel within the area is eligible for tax relief;

- where an employee lives outside his or her area, travel to the start of the area is classified as home-to-work travel and is taxable if paid for by the employer; or

- the entire country is likely to be the area for any employee whose duties extend to servicing customers throughout the whole of the UK.

All travelling appointments of service engineers are treated as business travel qualifying for tax relief.

(c) More than one workplace

No tax relief is due for travel from home to either place of work for employees with more than one permanent place of location. It is HMRC's view that a workplace is likely to be considered as permanent if:

- an employee regularly performs 40% or more of the duties of the employment there;

- customers, suppliers and others would expect to make contact with the employee there; and

- the employee has an office, or desk, and support services.

Home working

A growing number of people are now giving up the daily commute in favour of working from home, either full-time or on a part-time basis. This is being made increasingly possible because of modern technology.

However, to get tax benefits, you must be able to demonstrate that you work from home as a necessity rather than by choice. If you satisfy this test you should be able to claim tax relief on:

- a proportion of your household costs such as heating, lighting, telephone and water (if any);

- use of your car, computer and tools for your employer's business; and

- other expenses you incur on stationery, books and professional subscriptions for the business.

Benefits-in-kind

Employees (including full-time working directors who own 5% or under of the company's shares) earning less than £8,500 per annum, including expenses, are not taxed on most benefits or perks provided by their employers. In addition to the list of tax-free expenses, the most valuable non-taxable benefits for this class of employee are private medical insurance and a company car.

Other directors and employees (including full-time working directors), whose total earnings, including expenses, exceed £8,500 per annum, are generally taxed on the actual value of any employment-related benefits and taxable expenses. Information about your expense payments and benefits-in-kind is supplied by your employer to your Tax Office each year on a Form P11D. Your employer should give you a copy of this form by 6 July following the end of the tax year. It sets out your employer's calculations of your taxable payments and cash equivalents of benefits-in-kind. It is up to you to claim those that are not taxable. This should not cause you any problem where expenses such as travelling and entertaining have genuinely arisen from the performance of the duties of your employment.

There are set rules for calculating some benefits.

(a) Company cars

The tax charge is based on a percentage of the list price of a car (subject to a ceiling of £80,000) but graduated according to the level of the car's carbon dioxide (CO_2) emissions. The minimum charge is 15% of list price, increasing to a maximum of 35% if CO_2 emissions are above the prescribed level.

In view of their higher emissions of pollutants diesel cars are subject to a 3% supplementary charge. However, even for diesel cars the maximum charge cannot exceed 35% of a car's price.

The car benefit charges for cars with an approved CO_2 emissions figure for the 2006/07 and 2007/08 years are as follows:

CO_2 emissions in g/km	% of list price which is taxed	
	Petrol	*Diesel*
140	15	18
145	16	19
150	17	20
155	18	21
160	19	22
165	20	23
170	21	24
175	22	25
180	23	26
185	24	27
190	25	28
195	26	29
200	27	30

CO_2 emissions in g/km	% of list price which is taxed	
	Petrol	Diesel
205	28	31
210	29	32
215	30	33
220	31	34
225	32	35
230	33	35
235	34	35
240	35	35

The regime extends to all cars, not just new ones. However, special rules apply to:

- older cars (those registered before 1 January 1998); and

- cars first registered on or after 1 January 1998 with no CO_2 emissions.

Cars first registered before 1 January 1998 will have no CO_2 emissions figures and, therefore, the taxable car benefit is worked out on a percentage of list price based on engine size:

Engine size	% of list price which is taxed
Up to 1,400	15
1,401–2,000	22
2,001 or more	32

The same applies to cars registered on or after 1 January 1998 with no CO_2 emissions figures, as follows:

Engine size	% of list price which is taxed
Up to 1,400	15 (18% if diesel)
1,401–2,000	25 (28% if diesel)
2,001 or more	35

For an electrically propelled car the percentage limit is 9%, and for a car with no cylinder capacity it is 35%.

Mileage between home and work counts as private, not business, usage except in a car made available to an employee who:

- has a travelling appointment; or

- travels from home to a temporary place of work and the distance travelled is less than the distance between the normal place of work and the temporary place of work; or

- is a home worker and travels from home to another place of work in the performance of his or her duties.

There are several other circumstances where home-to-work travel in an employer-provided car is considered to be private use but is disregarded for tax purposes. These are where the car is provided:

- to a disabled person for home-to-work travel and there is no other private use;

- for home-to-work travel when public transport is disrupted; and

- for late-night journeys home from work.

(b) Fuel benefits

If your employer pays for fuel for your private motoring this also gives rise to a taxable benefit on which you have to pay Income Tax. The taxable amount is calculated on the car benefit percentage for the CO_2 emissions of your car multiplied by 14,400, giving the following taxable benefits for the 2006/07 tax year:

CO_2 emissions in g/km	% of list price which is taxed		Taxable benefit (£)	
	Petrol	Diesel	Petrol	Diesel
145	15	18	2,160	2,592
150	16	19	2,304	2,736
155	17	20	2,448	2,880
160	18	21	2,592	3.024
165	19	22	2,736	3,168
170	20	23	2,880	3,312
175	21	24	3,024	3,456
180	22	25	3,168	3,600
185	23	26	3,312	3,744
190	24	27	3,456	3,888
195	25	28	3,600	4,032
200	26	29	3,744	4,176
205	27	30	3,888	4,320
210	28	31	4,032	4,464
215	29	32	4,176	4,608
220	30	33	4,320	4,752
225	31	34	4,464	4,896
230	32	35	4,608	5,040
235	33	35	4,752	5,040
240	34	35	4,896	5,040
245	35	35	5,040	5,040

The benefit is:

- reduced to zero if the full cost of fuel for all your private motoring is reimbursed to your employer;

- proportionately reduced if you stop enjoying the use of free fuel for non-business motoring partway through a tax year; and

- not charged for any period of at least 30 days during which your car cannot be used or is unavailable to you.

(c) Company vans

If your employer provides you with a company van, with a gross vehicle weight not exceeding 3,500 kilograms, for private travel the rules are as follows:

- you are taxed on a fixed amount of £500 for a van which is less than four years old at the end of the tax year;

- the tax charge is worked out on a lower figure of £350 for an older van;

- there is no taxable benefit if you just take your van home and there is no other private use.

There is no taxable benefit on the incidental private use of a heavy commercial vehicle with a design weight exceeding 3,500 kilograms.

From 6 April 2007 the fixed taxable scale charge increases to £3,000 no matter the age of the van. Where there is unrestricted private use tax is also payable on a fuel charge of £500.

(d) Pooled vehicles

The private use of a car or van from an employer's pool of vehicles will not give rise to a tax charge on an employee provided:

- any home-to-work travel is merely incidental to business use; and

- the vehicle is not garaged at or near the employee's home overnight.

(e) Living accommodation

In some trades it is established practice for an employer to provide living accommodation. This can also be desirable where there is a security risk. No Income Tax liability arises in either set of circumstances.

In other situations Income Tax is chargeable on the annual value of the property after deducting any rent paid for it. For these purposes the annual valuation is broadly equivalent to the gross rateable value. Estimated rateable values will be used for new properties not appearing on the domestic rating list.

An additional tax charge arises where the accommodation costs more than £75,000. This is worked out by applying HMRC's official interest rate (see below) to the excess of the cost price above £75,000.

(f) Beneficial loans

The rules dealing with interest-free or low-rate-interest loans from an employer are as follows:

- the taxable benefit is worked out by applying HMRC's official rate of interest to the loan, which is 5% for the 2006/07 tax year;

- any interest actually paid on the loan reduces the amount of the benefit;

- no tax charge arises where all of an employee's cheap or interest-free loans, excluding loans that qualify for tax relief, total less than £5,000;

- there is no tax charge where the loan is for a purpose on which the interest would qualify for tax relief (see Chapter 4).

(g) Medical insurance

You will be taxed on the cost of private medical insurance premiums paid by your employer for you or other members of your family. Not subject to tax is the cost of medical insurance cover, or actual medical treatment overseas, while away on business.

(h) Relocation expenses

An employee who changes his job, or is relocated by his employer, is not taxed on the costs of a relocation package up to £8,000. This limit applies to each job-related move. There are specific definitions for the removal expenses and benefits that qualify for exemption within the monetary limit.

Employee share ownership

There are a variety of share, profit sharing and share option schemes, all offering different investment limits and tax reliefs – some more generous than others.

(a) Under an All-Employee Share Scheme:

- employers can give employees up to £3,000 of shares free of Income Tax and National Insurance;

- some or all of these shares can be awarded to employees for reaching performance targets;

- employees are able to buy partnership shares out of their pre-tax salary or wage up to a maximum of 10% of salary or £1,500 a year, free of Income Tax and National Insurance;

- employers can match partnership shares by giving employees up to two free shares for each partnership share they buy;

- employees who sell their shares are liable to Capital Gains Tax only on any increase in the value of their shares after they come out of a plan;

- free and matching shares must normally be kept in the plan for at least three years – employees can take partnership shares out of the plan at any time;

- shares must come out of the plan when employees leave and some employees may lose their free and matching shares if they leave their jobs within three years of getting the shares;

- dividends, up to £1,500 annually, paid on the shares are tax free providing they are reinvested in additional shares in the company and retained for at least three years;

- employees who keep their shares in a plan for five years pay no Income Tax or National Insurance on those shares;

- employees who take their shares out of a plan after three years pay Income Tax and National Insurance on no more than the initial value of the shares – any increase in the value of their shares while in the plan is free of Income Tax and National Insurance; and

- Capital Gains Tax roll-over relief is available for existing shareholders of smaller companies who want to sell their shares to a new plan trust to be used for the benefit of employees.

(b) The main features of a Savings-Related Share Option Scheme are:

- it operates in combination with either a bank or building society SAYE savings contract under which employees save a fixed regular amount each month;

- the maximum amount that can be saved is £250 per month over either a three or five-year period;

- the price at which options can be offered to directors and employees cannot be less than 80% of the market value of the shares at the time the options are granted; and

- the receipt of the options and any increase in the value of the shares between the time that the options are granted and the date when they are exercised are free of Income Tax.

(c) Under an Approved Profit-Sharing Scheme:

- a company makes an allocation of profits to Trustees who, in turn, use the contribution in acquiring shares in the company which are subsequently allotted to employees;

- the limit on the market value of shares which may be appropriated to any one individual in each tax year is 10% of salary with a minimum limit of £3,000 and a maximum of £8,000; and

- there is no Income Tax liability when the shares are set aside or if they are retained by the Trustees of the scheme for three years.

(d) Inland Revenue Approved Share Option Plan:

- no liability to Income Tax is imposed on a director or employee who acquires, or disposes of, ordinary shares under such a plan;

- the market value of shares, at the time of the grant of the option, over which an individual holds unexercised rights under the plan must not exceed £30,000;

- an option must be exercised not less than three, or more than ten, years after it is granted, or under three years after a previous exercise;

- the gain is measured by the difference between the sale proceeds and the cost of acquiring the shares, and is charged to Capital Gains Tax at the time of disposal; and

- the price payable must be fixed at the time of the grant and must not be less than the market value of the shares at that date.

Enterprise Management Incentives

Enterprise Management Incentives are aimed at:

- helping small companies attract and retain the key people they need; and

- rewarding employees for taking a risk by investing their time and skills in helping small companies achieve their potential.

Normally, without any charge to Income Tax or National Insurance, companies can grant share options to employees worth up to £100,000 at the time of the grant. Moreover, when the shares are sold, the ownership period for Capital Gains Tax taper relief usually starts from the date when the options are granted.

A qualifying employee is one who must spend at least 25 hours a week, or if less, 75% of their working time on the business of that company.

Payments on termination of employment

It is often the practice for an employee to be paid a lump sum on the termination of an employment. If the right to receive the lump sum arose during the employment then it is taxable in full in the same way as any other earnings. Otherwise the lump sum payment is either wholly or partly tax free. Such payments are free of tax where:

- the employment ceases because of the accidental death, injury or disability of the employee; or

- most of the employee's time was spent working overseas for the employer.

Where the lump sum payment is made at a time other than on death or retirement, then the first £30,000 is tax free. It is only the excess of any payment over £30,000 that is taxable.

Any statutory redundancy repayment you receive, although it is itself exempt from tax, has to be added to any other lump sum payment from your employer in working out the Income Tax due on the amount.

It is not unusual for redundancy and employment termination settlements to provide for benefits, such as membership of a company medical insurance scheme, to continue after the employment has come to an end. Such payments and benefits are taxed only to the extent that they actually arise, and in the year in which they are received or enjoyed.

Belinda Morrison was made redundant in May 2006. Under her employment termination settlement she received lump sum payments of £26,000 and £20,000 on 25 May 2006 and 12 April 2007 respectively. She was also permitted to retain her membership of her employer's company medical insurance scheme for four years at an annual cost to her employer of £1,000. Belinda's total redundancy package for 2006/07 comes to £27,000. As this is below the £30,000 exemption limit she does not pay tax on any part of the package she received in 2006/07. The balance of the exemption limit of £3,000 is carried forward to 2007/08 to be set against the cash payment of £20,000 and the medical insurance benefit of £1,000. For 2007/08, therefore, Belinda's old employer will deduct tax at the basic rate of 22% on £18,000.

6 VALUE ADDED TAX

Value Added Tax (VAT) is a system for taxing what people spend. It is also administered by HMRC. The National Advice Service (NAS) is the main contact point for businesses. The NAS telephone number is 0845 010 9000.

What is VAT?

VAT is a self-assessed tax charged on:

- the supply of goods and services in the UK; and

- the import of goods and certain services into the UK.

It applies where a taxable person in business makes supplies which are taxable supplies.

Rates of VAT

There are three rates of VAT: a standard rate of 17.5%, a reduced rate of 5% and a zero rate. Most of the goods and services supplied in the UK are liable to tax at the standard rate. Among the goods and services liable at the two lower rates are:

- Supplies charged at 5%:
  - domestic fuel and power
  - renovations and alterations of dwellings
  - residential conversions
- Zero-rated supplies:
  - food sold in shops
  - books and newspapers
  - children's clothing and footwear
  - construction of new houses

— passenger transport

— exports of goods

Exempt supplies

Some goods and services have no VAT on them. These include:

* Exempt supplies:

  — education

  — health and welfare

  — insurance

  — land

  — finance and banking transactions

If you sell goods or supply services which are exempt you do not charge VAT, but neither can you recover VAT charged on the purchases and expenses of your business. Special rules apply where your business makes both chargeable and exempt supplies.

Registration

If you are just starting up a business it is unlikely you will need to register for VAT immediately. Only when the value of your taxable supplies reaches £61,000 in a 'rolling' 12-month period is it compulsory to apply for registration. In working out the turnover of your business for this purpose remember that taxable supplies are not just those liable at the standard rate of 17.5% but include supplies liable to tax at the lower rates of 5% and zero.

Simon Potter started up in business in August 2005. He has been successful in building up his turnover each month. Looking back from the end of January 2007 his turnover for the previous twelve months was £57,000. But when he did the same exercise a month later this figure had increased to £63,000. Simon had to notify liability to register by 31 March 2007 and was registered for VAT from 1 April 2007.

You also need to register if the taxable supplies of your business are likely to exceed the registration limit of £61,000 in the next 30 days. Also, do not delay making an application for registration if you acquire an existing business where the previous owner was VAT registered. Sometimes it is possible for you to take on the same registration number as that of the previous owner.

You can only avoid registration if you can satisfy HMRC that either:

- your taxable turnover is expected to decline so that, from then on, it will remain at an annual level under £59,000; or

- your business activities are such that, if registration was in place, you would normally receive repayments of VAT.

Form VAT1 has to be used to register for VAT. You can normally expect to receive your VAT number within 15 working days. You can help the registration process by:

- applying for your registration in good time;

- ensuring that your application is complete and accurate; and

- sending your application to the correct address which is governed by your postcode.

Your formal certificate of registration will follow a week or two after you have received the letter advising you of your VAT number. You will probably also be sent one or two leaflets of a general nature. There may be other information which would be of benefit to you and your business. Appendix 3 at the end of the book lists some of the VAT notices currently available from the NAS.

Voluntary registration

Sometimes there are benefits from VAT registration even though the turnover of your business is below the compulsory limit for registration. Voluntary registration is allowed providing you can show that you are, or will be, making some taxable supplies.

An advantage of voluntary registration is that you can reduce your costs by recovering VAT incurred on your business expenses, including VAT paid on certain start-up costs and on the acquisition of assets such as computers and printers.

But if your customers are the general public, voluntary registration is not likely to be beneficial. They cannot recover the VAT charged on your goods and services so you may be putting yourself at a price disadvantage compared to your competitors.

Cancellation of registration

You can apply to HMRC to deregister your business from VAT:

- where the taxable turnover in the previous year was below the registration threshold of £61,000; or

- the anticipated turnover in the coming 12 months will be below £59,000.

Deregistration is compulsory where:

- you cease to trade; or

- you sell your business.

Help from HMRC

It is the policy of HMRC to try and make contact with new businesses soon after they have become registered so that:

- Any queries which may already have arisen can be resolved.

- You can be offered videos on various aspects of the tax, an opportunity to attend a seminar or, alternatively, a one-to-one meeting to discuss matters of a more individual nature.

- The advantages of the simplication measures available to smaller businesses can be pointed out to you.

It is unusual these days for HMRC to take a hard-line approach when smaller businesses, new to VAT, run into difficulties in preparing their first one or two VAT Returns or paying the tax shown to be due. Any initial difficulties are, however, expected to be only short-term.

If you have an enquiry of a technical nature I suggest you set out the details in a letter to HMRC. The NAS will let you have the address of the office to which you should write.

VAT invoices

There are a number of items which you must show on all VAT invoices issued by your business. These mandatory requirements are:

- the date of issue;

- a sequential number which uniquely identifies the invoice;

- your VAT identification number;

- the full name and address of both your own business and that of your customer;

- the quantity and nature of the goods supplied or services rendered;

- the tax point;

- the net unit price;

- the rate of VAT charged; and

- the amount of VAT payable.

There are also other specific requirements but these only apply in certain circumstances such as supplies to and from other EU countries.

You are also allowed to issue invoices electronically. Furthermore you can agree with your customers that they will raise the invoices for the goods or services you have supplied to them. This practice is known as self-billing.

Records, accounting and returns

If your business is VAT registered you must:

- render tax invoices for all taxable supplies of goods and services;

- maintain an account showing the calculations of your VAT liability for each VAT period; and

- make timely VAT Returns to HMRC.

The VAT payable, or repayable, each period is the simple difference between your VAT output tax and input tax. Output tax is what you charge on the goods and services (outputs) to your customers. Input tax is what you incur on the purchases and expenses (inputs) of running your business. You should keep copies of every invoice for all your sales and purchases which should be filed in an orderly manner.

Totalling the VAT on your outputs and inputs each month should make it fairly straightforward to bring together the information you need to complete the VAT Return – Form VAT100 – for the accounting periods shown on your registration certificate.

Beth Way runs a hairdressing salon which is VAT registered. She has been given quarterly VAT accounting periods in line with the calendar quarters. She accounts for VAT as a retailer on the basis of the income received each quarter. Her VAT account for the three months to the end of March 2007 was:

	£	£
Output Tax		
January	1,940	
February	1,830	
March	2,070	
Total	£5,840	5,840
Input Tax		
January	220	
February	160	
March	250	
Total	£630	630
Net amount due to HMRC		£5,210

The various boxes on your VAT Return can be filled in from the figures in your VAT account and the tax-exclusive values of your outputs and inputs for the period.

Make sure you submit each Return and pay what is due to HMRC within the stipulated time limit. If the VAT you have reclaimed on the purchases and expenses of the business exceeds the VAT on your turnover for the period, the Return will show you are entitled to a repayment which will be sent direct to your bank account.

If you wish, you can request that your quarterly VAT Return periods coincide with your financial year.

Alternatively you can submit your VAT Return electronically. If you do so you must also pay any VAT due by direct debit.

Input tax

The actual amount of input tax on purchases does not matter quite so much when the Flat Rate Scheme is used; see page 59. For other businesses it is only the input tax on the costs of the business which can be claimed when VAT Returns are completed. Sometimes expenses may be incurred where input tax cannot be claimed at all. Examples are business entertaining and private purchases paid for through your business. Occasionally there may be a need to apportion input tax, such as that on home telephone bills which are partly for business and partly for private purposes. Apportionment is best done on a percentage basis which, provided it is reasonable, HMRC can be expected to accept.

Motor cars and fuel

Businesses directly concerned with motoring, like new car dealers, vehicle hirers, taxi drivers or driving schools, may be able to reclaim all input tax on cars which they buy or lease. Input tax cannot be claimed back on cars bought by other businesses and made available for private use. However, it may be possible to claim 50% of the input tax on the rental payments where cars are leased.

There are two alternative methods for dealing with input tax on motor fuel, namely:

- all input tax is claimed and a quarterly fixed-scale charge to take account of private use is applied in accordance with the following table:

	Diesel		Petrol	
Engine Size	*Scale Charge*	*VAT*	*Scale Charge*	*VAT*
cc	*£*	*£*	*£*	*£*
1,400 or less	260	38.72	273	40.66

Engine Size	Diesel		Petrol	
	Scale Charge	VAT	Scale Charge	VAT
cc	£	£	£	£
1,401 to 2,000	260	38.72	346	51.53
Over 2,000	331	49.30	508	75.66

- no input tax is claimed and the fixed-scale charge is ignored.
  If you intend to deal with motor fuel this way you should write to
  HMRC to tell them.

Input tax on repairs and maintenance of business cars can be claimed
whichever way you decide to deal with motor fuel.

Bad debts

Late or non-payment of bills can often have a serious impact on both the
cash flow and profitability of a business. When it comes to bad debts it
is only when a debt is more than six months old that an adjustment can
be made to recover VAT accounted for on that debt in a previous VAT
Return.

Adjustments for bad debts, although not separately shown on VAT
Returns, must be recorded separately in the VAT account of your business. Listings must be maintained both to support the entries and any
further adjustments made to reflect subsequent payments received.

Special schemes for retailers

Retailers often sell a mixture of both positive and zero-rated goods but
do not know how much of each of them is sold from day to day. When
this happens they can use one of the schemes available to help them
work out their VAT liabilities. If you are in retailing you should study the
leaflets telling you about the various schemes so that you do not pay too
much tax.

Where retailers only sell goods which are liable at the standard rate of
17.5%, the amount of tax included in the gross takings for a period is
$7/47$. Referred to as the 'VAT fraction' this calculation is worked out as
follows:

	£
Tax-exclusive value (say)	100.00
Add: VAT @ 17.5%	17.50
Tax-inclusive price	£117.50

The VAT included in the tax-inclusive price is therefore:

$$\frac{17.5}{117.5} = \frac{7}{47}$$

For goods liable at the reduced rate of 5% the 'VAT fraction' is $1/21$.

Where a retailer makes a supply for more than £250 the business must issue a proper tax invoice when asked to do so. For supplies under £250 there is usually enough information on till receipts for the 'VAT fraction' to be worked out by customers who, in the course of their business, make retail purchases and want to claim back the input tax suffered.

Flat Rate Scheme

The scheme is open to small businesses whose annual taxable turnover (not including VAT) does not exceed £150,000. It will be of particular appeal to businesses which do not want to spend too much time and effort dealing with all the administrative complications of normal VAT accounting. Under the scheme, VAT is still charged to customers at the rate appropriate to the supplies made by the business. When you come to complete your VAT Returns:

- you do not make a separate claim to recover input tax on purchases, expenses or low-value assets acquired for your business;

- any input tax on capital assets with a value of more than £2,000 may be claimable separately; and

- you work out the tax due by applying a fixed percentage to the VAT inclusive turnover of your business for the period.

The percentages have been set by HMRC according to the principal activity of a business and take into account that input tax on normal purchases is not claimed.

Yvonne Spencer is a photographer. Her VAT inclusive turnover for the most recent VAT period was £18,000. Yvonne must pay VAT of £1,710 as follows:

£18,000 x 9.5% = £1,710

Businesses are being strongly encouraged by HMRC to use the scheme, so much so that a 1% reduction in the percentages for the first year is available to new businesses:

- that register for VAT when they should; and

- apply to use the scheme at the same time.

Cash accounting

Under the cash accounting scheme:

- you account for VAT on your outputs when you are paid for sales made by your business, rather than by reference to the date of your tax invoices; and

- you reclaim the VAT on your purchases and business expenses when you pay for them.

Your business is eligible to use this scheme from the beginning of a VAT tax period if:

- you expect the value of your taxable supplies (excluding VAT) during the forthcoming year to be no more than £660,000; and

- you are not in arrears in submitting past VAT Returns at the time you decide to join the scheme.

You must come out of cash accounting if:

- the amount of your taxable supplies exceeds £825,000 (exclusive of VAT) in a period of one year; or

- your business fails to comply with the correct requirements for record keeping.

Annual accounting

Under the annual accounting scheme your business:

- submits just one VAT Return each year;
- makes interim payments of VAT based on an estimate of your liability for the year; and
- completes and sends in its VAT Return two months after the end of the year. At the same time you pay over the balance of VAT due.

You can apply to use the scheme if:

- your business has been VAT registered for under a year and there are good grounds for thinking that the annual taxable turnover will be less than £150,000; or
- your business has been VAT registered for over a year and the annual value of your supplies is more than £150,000 but less than £1.35 million.

These turnover tests are tax-exclusive. If you are accepted on to the scheme the start date for the new arrangements will be the first day of your current accounting period. You will be notified in writing if your application has been accepted. The letter you receive will also tell you:

- the amount and timing of your interim payments; and
- the due date of the Annual Return and balancing payment.

Vince Charles is in business as a vehicle repairer and is registered for VAT. In October 2006 he applies to use the annual accounting scheme. His quarterly period runs from 1 September to 30 November. His first annual accounting period starts on 1 September 2006 and ends on 31 August 2007.

Once you are in the scheme you can remain in it until your annual turnover exceeds £1.6 million. You will then be taken off the scheme at the end of your current accounting year. Alternatively, if you want to come out of the scheme and go back to the normal method of paying and accounting for VAT you just need to tell HMRC of your decision.

Penalties, surcharges and interest

It is extremely important for a new business to keep an eye on how turnover is progressing as there is a scaled penalty for not registering on time. The penalty is based on the net tax due beginning with the date:

- registration for VAT should have started to the day your VAT1 Form is received by HMRC; or

- liability to be registered is discovered.

The rates of penalty are as follows:

Registration not more than 9 months late	5%
Registration over 9 months, but not more than 18 months, late	10%
Registration more than 18 months late	15%

There is a minimum penalty of £50 and the back tax must also be paid, although it might be possible to do so in stages.

There are other penalties for businesses which are not careful with their VAT records, declarations and payments. You should aim to declare and pay the true amount of VAT in each and every period. Getting it right first time is best for everyone. Of course, errors are always possible, although they may be innocent.

Any errors taken together that involve VAT of less than £2,000 can be adjusted in the Return for a current quarter. However, if the total of any errors exceeds £2,000:

- spotting where they have been made;

- what they amount to; and

- owning up

means that it may be possible to avoid incurring a misdeclaration penalty. You should use Form VAT652 to notify HMRC of errors greater than £2,000. Alternatively you can send in a letter with details of the errors you have discovered. The misdeclaration penalty is a flat 15%. Whether or not it is imposed depends very much upon the correct amounts of output and input tax that should have been declared for the period. Furthermore, default interest, currently at the rate of 7.5% per annum, will normally be charged when assessments for errors are issued.

If you persistently keep making mistakes with VAT you may incur yet a further penalty. But you can apply to get it reduced.

Surcharges can be imposed by HMRC where you fail to:

- file your VAT Returns with the VAT Central Unit at Southend-on-Sea on time; and/or

- pay the proper amount of tax when it is due.

Default surcharges range from 2% to 15% where a history of default has built up. Surcharge assessments are, however, seldom issued unless they are calculated to exceed £200.

HMRC will pay you interest, currently at the rate of 4%, in cases where they make an official error.

Appeals

If you disagree with an officer's assessment or wish to appeal against a penalty or surcharge you can ask for the matter to be reconsidered. Someone other than the officer who issued the assessment or penalty should carry out the review. Alternatively you can lodge an appeal for a hearing before an independent VAT Tribunal. Lodging an appeal does not stop you from continuing a dialogue with HMRC in the hope of reaching a settlement without the need for a Tribunal hearing. The outcome of a Tribunal appeal very much depends upon the reasons why mistakes were made in the first place. Innocence is not normally accepted as an excuse.

Complaints

VAT officers are committed to the same standards as Tax staff, see the Service Commitment reproduced in Chapter 1, and are expected to abide by them. If you ever feel dissatisfied with the manner in which the affairs of your business have been handled, or that an officer has overstepped the mark and has exceeded his authority, you can write to:

- the person who is in overall charge at the HMRC office for your business; or

- the Complaints Unit for the area where your business is situated.

If you are unable to resolve your complaint satisfactorily your next step is to contact the Adjudicator's Office, which is the independent body set up specifically for this purpose.

7 WORKING FOR YOURSELF

If you run your own business, other than through a company or in partnership, you are classified as self-employed for tax purposes. Your business might be a trade, profession or vocation.

Am I self-employed?

The main distinguishing factor between having self-employed status and working as an employee is the existence of a 'master–servant' relationship. Sometimes it is difficult to draw a line between:

- employment (a contract for service); and

- self-employment (a contract for services).

Your business will have the trappings of self-employment if you:

- are paid a fixed fee, rather than by the hour;

- have no entitlement to paid holidays or sick leave;

- are responsible for any losses arising out of your services or the goods you supply;

- can decide how, when and where the work should be undertaken;

- can dictate the hours you work; and

- provide your own tools.

You do not have to formalize any business relationship by entering into a contract for the supply of goods or services. Nevertheless, having a contract makes sound business sense because it will include matters other than those just relative to the taxation consequences of the relationship.

Starting up in business

Your business is now up and running. It is important that you quickly learn what you need to do about Tax, National Insurance (see Chapter 8) and maybe Value Added Tax (see Chapter 6). The best starting point is to telephone HMRC on 08459 15 45 15 and ask for a copy of their booklet 'Starting up in Business'. Reading it will help you understand what you need to know about keeping proper records of all your business transactions. It also covers other matters relevant to the self-employed taxpayer.

With the booklet comes Form CWF1 which you must complete to register for Tax and National Insurance. If you do not notify HMRC of your self-employment within three months after the end of the month in which you started up your business you will be liable to a fixed penalty of £100.

Records

I strongly recommend that you maintain a separate bank account for all your business income, purchases and expenses. As a minimum you should keep the following books of account, either manually or on computer:

- a cash book to record and analyse your sales and other receipts, purchases and overhead expenses which pass through your bank account; and

- a petty cash book to log all small transactions paid for in cash.

If you run a larger business you will probably need to keep other books of account as well. Whatever the size of your business it is a good discipline to write up all your books of account on a regular basis.

Furthermore, in order that you comply with the requirements for Self-Assessment, you should keep and file the following:

- invoices for sales made by your business;

- bank statements and paying-in slips to show where the income comes from;

- invoices for goods acquired or costs incurred;

- documentation supporting purchases and sales of assets used in your business; and

- records in support of amounts taken out of the business for personal use (drawings) and all money paid into your business from personal funds (capital introduced).

Accounts

You can choose the date to which you draw up the accounts of your self-employment each year. For this reason it is unlikely that the first accounts will cover a full year of the activities of your business. You can make up your accounts from the date you start in business to the end of:

- a particular month;

- your first year's trading;

- the calendar year on 31 December; or

- the tax year on 5 April.

Thereafter you should continue to draw up your accounts to the same date every year. You are allowed to change this date where you can show good reason to do so.

Your accounts should be drawn up to:

- work out the profit earned or loss sustained in the financial period; and

- summarize, whenever possible, on the balance sheet the amounts of the assets and liabilities at the year-end.

The statement of the profit or loss of your business is not usually the simple difference between receipts and payments. For example, if you sell to customers on credit there will inevitably be some unpaid sales at the year-end. These outstanding invoices need to come into your accounts as income for that period. Equally, where amounts are due to your suppliers for purchases or expenses at the end of your financial period these need to be included in the accounts as costs incurred in the period. If your business is:

- One which requires you to keep a stock of raw materials or finished goods, the value of that stock at the year-end must be included in the profit and loss statement as income. The basis of valuation is cost or, in the case of redundant or old stock, realizable value. The amount of your stock at the beginning of the accounting period is deductible as a cost.

- Of a professional nature or you are a service provider you must also make an adjustment to your accounts at the end of each accounting period. You must bring in as income an amount in respect of ongoing, but unbilled, work by reference to the proportion of the work completed.

When it comes to expenses make sure you claim all the overhead costs. For example:

- If you are married or live with a partner and your spouse/partner helps you in the business by doing your accounts and acting as a part-time secretary or assistant you can claim the salary paid to him/her as a business expense. You should pay a proper amount for these services. If this is his or her only job or income and the wage is less than £5,035 for the year then there will be no tax or National Insurance to pay.

- If some of the paperwork from your business is done at home you can include a proportion of your home expenses, such as light, heat and insurance as a deduction in your accounts.

There will be some costs of your business, such as a car used both privately and for work, when it may be difficult to apportion the expenditure between the private and business elements. Where there is this overlap I suggest you include a note in the additional information section of the self-employed pages of your Tax Return so your Tax Office can see how you have worked out the percentage of the expenditure chargeable to the business.

Dennis Cole started his business of supplying and fitting carpets back in August 2000. He has a shop in his local high street which he rents. His wife keeps his accounts, prepares his VAT Returns and helps part-time in the shop.

Dennis makes up his accounts to 31 July each year. The statement of his business income and expenses for the financial year to 31 July 2006 is as follows:

		£	£	£
Sales				340,540
Less:	Cost of sales			
	Stock of carpets and other materials at start of year		28,100	
	Purchases during the year		179,100	
			207,200	

Less:	Stock of carpets and other materials at end of year		31,350	175,850

Gross Profit 164,690

Less: Overhead expenses

	Wages of shop assistants and fitters		62,860
	Shop expenses		
	Rent	15,000	
	Business and water rates	3,340	
	Light and heat	2,965	
	Cleaning	2,100	
	Insurance	1,640	
	Window repairs	385	
			25,430
Wife's salary			4,500
Printing, postage and stationery			3,630
Shop telephone and fax			1,380
Advertising and promotion			5,220
Van expenses			4,070
Entertaining			240
Accountancy			2,200
Legal Fees – new lease			1,100
Car expenses			
Road Fund Licence and Insurance		560	
Petrol and oil		1,410	
Repairs and servicing		620	
		2,590	
Business proportion	30%	777	
Use of home as office	($1/7$ x £2,450)	350	
Home telephone	(25%)	280	
Bank interest and charges		2,403	
Staff welfare		630	
Miscellaneous expenses		860	
			115,930

Profit for the year £48,760

Nowadays, annual accounts of a business are often needed for reasons other than tax. For example:

- to verify income in support of an application for a mortgage; or

- by your bank manager when weighting up an application for a business loan or overdraft facility.

Tax Return information

If you were in business at any time during the 2006/07 tax year you will need to complete the supplementary self-employment pages to accompany your Tax Return for the year. The self-employment pages are in a set format for reporting the annual income and expenses of your business, providing the turnover is more than £15,000 annually. Your Return will not be accepted as complete if the information about your business income and expenses is not presented in the required format.

When Dennis Cole comes to complete the supplementary self-employment pages for the year ended 5 April 2007 he will fill in the section on business income and expenses, based on his accounts for the financial year to 31 July 2006, as follows:

		£	£
Sales/business income (excluding VAT)			340,540
Less:	Cost of sales	175,850	
	Other direct costs	—	
			175,850
Gross profit			164,690
Other income/profits			—
			164,690
Less:	*Expenses*		
	Employee costs	67,360	
	Premises costs	25,395	
	Repairs	385	
	General administrative expenses	5,290	
	Motor expenses	4,847	
	Travel and subsistence	630	
	Advertising, promotion and entertainment	5,460	
	Legal and professional costs	3,300	
	Bad debts	—	

	£	£
Interest	2,403	
Other finance charges	—	
Depreciation and loss/(profit) on sale	—	
Other expenses	860	
Total expenses		115,930
Net profit		£48,760

Notes:

(1) Employee costs are:

Wages	62,860	
Wife's salary	4,500	
	£67,360	

(2) Premises costs are:

Shop expenses (excluding window repairs)	25,045	
Use of home as office	350	
	£25,395	

(3) General administrative expenses are:

Printing, postage and stationery	3,630	
Telephone (shop and home)	1,660	
	£5,290	

(4) Legal and professional costs are:

Accountancy	2,200	
Legal fees	1,100	
	£3,300	

So as to minimize the risk of HMRC raising enquiries into your self-employment income and Tax Return, you should adopt a consistent pattern from year-to-year in the way you analyse your business expenses under the various headings of the standardized format.

If the annual turnover of your business is less than £15,000 you can complete the special shortened income and expenses section at the foot of the first page of the self-employment supplement. This comprises a three-line statement of:

- turnover and other business receipts;
- business expenses allowable for tax; and
- resulting profit or loss.

Profits for tax

The profit disclosed by your business accounts will not necessarily be the same as that on which your tax bill is calculated. This is because certain types of expenditure are specifically not allowable in working out taxable business profits. These include:

- business entertainment;
- non-business charitable donations;
- amounts spent on items of a capital nature;
- professional costs related to capital expenditure; and
- general provisions and reserves.

Although Dennis Cole's accounts for his financial year to 31 July 2006 show he made a profit of £48,760, his taxable profit is £50,100 as follows:

	£	£
Profit as per accounts		48,760
Add: Disallowable expenses		
Entertainment	240	
Legal fees re new lease	1,100	
		1,340
Profit as adjusted for tax purposes		£50,100

Profits of the tax year

Self-employed individuals are taxed on the profits of their financial year ending in the tax year. This is known as 'the basis period'.

> The tax-adjusted profit of £50,100 for the year to 31 July 2006 of Dennis Cole's carpet business will be taxed in 2006/07.

There are special rules for working out the profits on which you pay tax in the opening years of your business, as follows:

- in the first tax year your taxable profits are those arising in the period from commencement to the following 5 April;

- if you choose to prepare your business accounts up to a date 12 months after you began your business then, in the second tax year, you pay tax on the profits for the first full year of trading; and

- for the third and all subsequent tax years you pay tax on the profits for 'the basis period'.

Under these rules it is usual for the profits for some periods of account to be taken into account more than once in working out the amount on which you pay tax. However, over the lifetime of your business it is intended that the profits should be taxed in full but once and once only. As a result, profits which are taxed more than once are eligible for a special relief. Known as overlap relief it will be given when either:

- a business ceases; or

- for any earlier tax year where the basis period exceeds 12 months.

> James Gray started up in business on 1 May 2006. His annual accounting date is 30 April. He makes the following profits in the first two years:
>
> | | |
> |---|---|
> | Year to 30.04.2007 | £24,720 |
> | Year to 30.04.2008 | £28,360 |
>
> The taxable profits for the first three tax years are:

Tax Year	Basis Period	Taxable Profit
		£
2006/07	01.05.2006 to 05.04.2007	22,660
2007/08	Year to 30.04.2007	24,720
2008/09	Year to 30.04.2008	28,360

On cessation the taxable profits for the final tax year will be:

- those earned in the period from the end of the basis period in the previous tax year up to cessation, but reduced by:

- overlap relief.

James Gray decides to close down his business on 30 April 2014. In the final year James makes profits of £34,950. The final tax year is 2014/15 and James will pay tax on:

		£
Taxable profit of final year		34,950
Less: Overlap	01.05.2006 to 05.04.2007	22,660
Net taxable amount		£12,290

Special rules apply when a business changes its accounting date. Apart from the first and last years of business the profits of a 12-month period are taxed in each tax year.

Sheila Windows began her business on 1 December 2006. She draws up her first accounts to 30 November 2007 and makes a profit of £33,000. She then decides to change her accounting date by extending it to 31 January 2009. The accounts for this 14-month period show a taxable profit of £28,000. Her basis period and taxable profits for the opening years of the business are:

Tax Year	Basis Period	Taxable Profit
		£
2006/07	01.12.2006 to 05.04.2007	11,000
2007/08	Year to 30.11.2007	33,000

The overlap period is from 01.12.2006 to 05.04.2007:

2008/09	01.12.2007 to 31.01.2009	
	(14 months)	28,000
Less: Overlap	01.12.2006 to 31.01.2007	5,500
		—————
Net taxable amount		£22.500

The overlap period was one of four months. As the accounting period from 1 December 2007 to 31 January 2009 is 14 months, the overlap is a period of two months. The amount deducted from the taxable profits for 2008/09 is half of the original overlap profit. A further two months of overlap relief is available either when the business ceases or in any subsequent tax year when the basis period is again longer than 12 months.

Post-cessation expenses

Tax relief is allowed on certain expenditure incurred after a business has ceased. The expenses which qualify for relief are those closely related to the trading or professional activities previously carried on but including, for example, relief for debts which have subsequently proved to be irrecoverable.

Relief is available for payments made within seven years of the permanent discontinuance of the business by setting the payments made against income for the same tax year. Any excess can be treated as a capital loss, but only of the same tax year.

Capital allowances

You can claim what are known as capital allowances on the expenditure you incur on items of a capital nature for your business.

Amounts spent by small businesses (your business is almost certain to qualify) attract the following rates of allowance in the first year:

* 50% where the investment is in information and communications

technology or for expenditure on plant, machinery, fixtures and fittings, but not motor cars;

- 100% for purchases of new low-emission cars for use by you or your staff in your business. To qualify a car must not emit more than 120 gm/km CO_2 or be electrically propelled; and

- 25% for other motor cars. There is a maximum allowance of £3,000 for cars costing more than £12,000.

In subsequent years your capital expenditure, after deducting your first year allowances, is further written down on the reducing-balance basis at the rate of 25% p.a. For cars, the maximum annual writing-down allowance is restricted to £3,000.

A separate 'pool' must be maintained for expenditure in each of the following different categories:

- all plant and equipment, including motor vans, lorries and cars costing up to £12,000;

- each car bought for over £12,000;

- each asset where there is both business and personal use; and

- each asset with a short life expectancy.

Where an asset on which capital allowances have been claimed is sold, you must bring the proceeds of sale into the computation of capital allowances. If it is sold:

- for less than the value to which it has been written-down for tax purposes you will probably be entitled to a further allowance equivalent to the difference between the sale proceeds and the written-down value; or

- for more than its written-down value then it is possible that the excess allowances will be clawed back in the year of sale.

These adjustments are respectively known as balancing allowances and balancing charges.

In his accounting year to 31 July 2006 Dennis Cole traded in his old car for £3,600 and bought a new one for £19,000. In the year he also spent £12,000 on a second-hand van, £1,500 on a computer and printer and £200 on a new filing cabinet. All these purchases were made after 31 March 2006. His claim to capital allowances for 2006/07, based on his capital expenditure in this year, is:

	£	Pool £	Car with Private Use £
Written-down values brought forward from 2005/06		6,300	4,100
Sale proceeds of car			3,600
Balancing allowance			500
Additions in the year:			
Van, computer and cabinet		13,700	
New car			19,000
		20,000	
Allowances due:			
First year – 50%	6,850		3,000
Writing down – 25%	1,575	8,425	
Carried forward to 2007/08		£11,575	£16,000
Summary of allowances:			
First year		9,850	
Writing down		1,575	
Balancing		500	
		11,925	
Less: 70% private use of car		2,450	
2006/07 Capital allowances		£9,475	

Capital allowances are deducted from your profits as a trading expense of your business. Any balancing charges are treated as an addition to your profit. It follows that:

- the chargeable period for the purposes of working out your capital allowances is the same as that for which you draw up your accounts; and

- the length of the period of account determines the amount of writing-down allowances to which you are entitled.

Thus, if a period of account:

- is only nine months long, 9/12th of the writing-down allowances can be deducted from taxable profits for that period; or

- extends to 15 months, the tax deductible allowances equal 15/12th of the writing-down allowances.

Should a period of account exceed 18 months it must be divided into one of 12 months and a balancing period with restricted writing-down allowances.

There is a section in the supplementary self-employment pages in which you must summarize your claim to capital allowances.

Losses

It is almost inevitable that your business will go through both good and bad times. If you incur a loss you can claim tax relief on the loss sustained as increased by the amount of your capital allowances for the same period. You can choose whether to set a trading loss against other income in either the same, or the preceding, tax year. But you cannot claim to relieve only part of a loss.

> Isabel Fletcher has been in business for many years. She makes up her accounts to 31 August each year. In the year ended 31 August 2007 she makes a loss which she can claim against her other income in 2007/08. Alternatively, the loss can be carried back and relieved against her total income in 2006/07.

Any relieved loss of your business then has to be carried forward for offset against profits from the same business in future years.

Alternatively you can claim to set a trading loss against capital gains (see Chapter 13) in the following way:

- the claim is for relief on the amount of the trading loss which cannot be set against your other income in the year or on which tax relief has already been given in some other way;

- the maximum loss eligible for relief against capital gains is the same as the amount of your gains chargeable to Capital Gains Tax, before taper relief is applied; and

- it is not possible to make a partial claim.

By relieving a business loss this way you may be wasting personal allowances as well as your annual exemption for Capital Gains Tax.

Tax relief for losses incurred by new businesses is extended such that:

- Losses incurred during the first four tax years can be set against your total income for the three years prior to that in which the loss arises.

- Relief is first of all given against total income for the earliest year. For example, if you set up in business during 2006/07 and sustained a loss in the first period of trading, that part of the loss attributable to the 2006/07 tax year can be set against your income in 2003/04, 2004/05 and 2005/06, beginning with 2003/04.

Sometimes you may have to spend monies on a new business venture before you actually start to trade. Any such expenditure incurred within seven years before trading begins is treated as a separate loss of the tax year in which trading commences.

There is one final type of loss relief which is only available to those businesses which incur a loss in their last period of trading. In such circumstances there cannot be future profits against which such a loss might be relieved. Therefore, a loss arising in the last 12 months of trading can be set back against the profits from the same business in both the final and three preceding tax years, beginning with the profits of the last year and working backwards.

Ralph Collins retires from business on 30 September 2007. In the final nine months in business he loses £18,000. Previously his business had always been successful as follows:

Accounting Year	Taxable Profits £	Year of Charge
Year ended 31 December 2003	16,000	2003/04
Year ended 31 December 2004	12,000	2004/05
Year ended 31 December 2005	9,000	2005/06
Year ended 31 December 2006	4,000	2006/07

The terminal loss can be set off as follows:

2006/07	4,000	leaving nil taxable profits
2007/08	9,000	leaving nil taxable profits
2008/09	5,000	reducing the taxable profits to £7,000
	£18,000	

Taking on staff

You have now reached the time where your business is expanding. You need an assistant or an extra pair of hands. At this stage get in contact with the Tax Office dealing with your business. The information you give will be sent to the right department since it is likely to be a different office to that dealing with your business. You should be sent a New Employer's Starter Pack containing all the instructions, tables and forms you need.

As an employer you are responsible for:

- working out the deductions for Income Tax (PAYE) and National Insurance contributions from the salary or wage paid to your employees at regular weekly or monthly intervals;

- paying over the deductions to the Collector of Taxes each month. These payments can be made every quarter where your average monthly payments of PAYE and National Insurance contributions are less than £1,500;

- letting your Tax Office know every year how much each employee has earned together with the deductions made for both Income Tax and National Insurance contributions. The deductions should reconcile to the total of the amounts paid over to the Collector of Taxes. You must also give details of any benefits paid or provided; and

- giving your employees certificates showing their earnings for the tax year, deductions for Income Tax and National Insurance contributions and the value of any benefits provided.

Foster carers

The self-employed who receive income from local authorities or independent fostering providers for providing foster care to children and young people are entitled to a special relief which comes in two parts:

- an exemption from Income Tax on receipts which do not exceed the qualifying amount for any year; and

- a simplified optional method of calculating taxable profits where receipts are more than the qualifying amount.

The annual qualifying amount is made up of two parts which must be added together. They are:

- a fixed amount for each household – £10,000 for 2006/07; and

- a weekly amount for each foster child placed with you – for 2006/07, £200 a week for a child under age 11 and £250 a week for a child over 11 years old.

Mollie Ford, who lives on her own, provides foster care for two boys during 2006/07. The 12-year-old is only with her for 16 weeks but the 9-year-old boy stays with her for the whole year. Her qualifying amount for 2006/07 is £24,400 calculated as follows:

	£
Fixed amount	10,000
9-year-old (52 weeks x £200)	10,400
12-year-old (16 weeks x £250)	4,000
2006/07 qualifying amount	£24,400

Where your receipts (fees, salaries, reward payments, allowances, etc) exceed the annual qualifying amount you can choose between paying tax on:

- your actual profits from foster caring worked out on the principles which apply for any other business; or

- profits worked out on a simplified method which is the difference between your total receipts for the year less the annual qualifying amount.

Whichever way you choose to be taxed you must at least keep records of your receipts and the ages and number of weeks that you care for each child placed with you. For this purpose a week runs from Monday to the following Sunday. Part of a week counts as a full week.

Furnished holiday accommodation

The letting of furnished holiday accommodation in the UK may be treated as a trade so long as the property is:

- let commercially and furnished;

- available for letting commercially to the public as holiday accommodation for at least 140 days in a 12-month period;

- actually let for at least 70 such days; and

- not normally occupied by the same person for more than 31 consecutive days at any time during the period of 7 months within the 12-month period.

As the letting of furnished holiday accommodation is treated as a trading activity:

- you can claim capital allowances on expenditure for furniture and equipment in the holiday home; and

- you can claim relief for losses against your other income.

Other special situations

In the space available I have only been able to paint a general picture of the way in which the profits of most businesses are taxed. If you are a farmer, a writer, a Lloyds underwriter or a subcontractor in the construction industry you should know that there are special rules for working out the taxable profits from these and some other trades, professions or vocations. In such situations it is advisable to seek professional assistance.

8 NATIONAL INSURANCE AND STATE BENEFITS

Employed or self-employed, you must pay National Insurance contributions as well as Income Tax on your earnings or business profits. By paying sufficient National Insurance contributions you become eligible to claim those social security benefits which are based on your contribution history. Many benefits, mainly those payable to the disabled, do not depend upon the payment of contributions.

National Insurance numbers

You need to have a National Insurance number (NINO) so that all the contributions you make can be properly recorded. All children whose parents were claiming Child Benefit for them at age 15 years and 9 months are automatically allocated a NINO. Otherwise you can apply at any time over age 16 providing you can satisfy the requirements of residence or presence in Great Britain.

Your NINO is made up of two letters, six numbers and followed by a further letter – A, B, C or D. You will receive a plastic card (an RD3), similar to a credit card, which will be sent to your home address.

National Insurance contributions

There are four classes of contribution payable as follows:

- Class 1 by employees;
- Class 2 by the self-employed;
- Class 3 which is voluntary; and
- Class 4 by the self-employed, based on profits.

You do not have to go on paying contributions once you have passed normal retirement age, currently 60 for a woman and 65 for a man, even if you carry on working either in employment or in your own business.

(a) Class 1

The earnings of employees on which contributions are calculated include:

- a salary or wage – before deduction for pension contributions;
- overtime, bonuses and commission;
- holiday pay; and
- statutory sick, maternity and paternity pay.

Nevertheless, no contributions are payable by employees on the cash equivalents of any benefits-in-kind such as a company car or medical insurance.

The contributions you pay are usually a percentage of your weekly or monthly salary or wage, subject to lower- and upper-earnings limits which change from year to year. If:

- you change jobs and have a break between them; or
- there is a period when you are unemployed.

The rate and amount of contribution you pay when you return to work is unaffected.

If you have more than one employment you must pay contributions on your earnings from all your jobs. However, there is an overall annual maximum limit of contributions payable by employees. You can apply for a refund in any year where the total contributions you have paid exceed this annual limit. Alternatively, by completing form CF379, you can apply for deferment where you reckon that the contributions you will pay on earnings from two or more employments will exceed the maximum annual limit. The Contributions Office of HMRC will then instruct one or other of your employers not to withhold contributions from your earnings. After the end of the tax year your overall contribution history is reviewed. If you have not paid enough contributions the Contributions Office will send you a calculation and a demand for the balance due.

(b) Class 2

This is a weekly flat rate payable by the self-employed. You can pay either by direct debit every four weeks or on demand every 13 weeks. If your business profits are less than a specified limit each year you are exempted from paying contributions. But you should apply in advance for what is known as small-earnings exception.

(c) Class 3

The payment of these flat-rate contributions is voluntary. They may be paid by a man under age 65 or a woman under 60 in order to preserve entitlement to a particular benefit such as the state pension.

(d) Class 4

These are payable by the self-employed based on a percentage of taxable business profits, after capital allowances, but before relief for pension contributions. They are paid each year through the tax system along with the Income Tax due on business profits.

The profits of Dennis Cole's business, as adjusted for tax purposes, are £50,100 for 2006/07. For the same year his claim to capital allowances amounts to £8,105, giving a net taxable amount of £41,995 for 2006/07. He pays Class 4 contributions of £2,364.95 as follows:

	£
On the first £5,035	Nil
On the next £28,505 @ 8%	2,280.40
On the next £8,455 @ 1%	84.55
	£2,364.95

(e) Rates and leaflets

The rates of National Insurance contributions for 2006/07 are listed in Appendix 4 at the end of the book.

Your local HMRC (National Insurance Contributions) office should be able to supply you with any leaflets or forms you need. A list of those with a wider application is in Appendix 5.

Social Security benefits

Responsibility for administering all aspects of the Social Security system lies with the Department for Work and Pensions (DWP). There are local

DWP offices all across the country. The framework of the social security system is now so substantial, and the range of benefits so wide and varied, it is only possible for me to give a brief summary of the main benefits.

Many benefits are only payable to individuals with an established National Insurance contribution history. The type of benefit you can claim depends on the class of contributions paid as follows:

Type of Benefit	Class 1 (Employed)	Class 2 (Self-Employed)	Class 3 (Voluntary)
Retirement Pension			
— basic	Yes	Yes	Yes
— additional	Yes	No	No
— widow's	Yes	Yes	Yes
Bereavement allowance	Yes	Yes	Yes
Bereavement payment	Yes	Yes	Yes
Widowed mother's allowance	Yes	Yes	Yes
Widowed parent's allowance	Yes	Yes	Yes
Widow's Payment	Yes	Yes	Yes
Incapacity benefit	Yes	Yes	No
Jobseeker's allowance	Yes	No	No
Statutory Sick, Maternity and Paternity Pay	Yes	No	No

Other benefits do not depend upon the payment of contributions.

(a) Statutory sick pay

To be able to claim statutory sick pay you must be paying sufficient Class 1 contributions. Other main points are:

- it is a flat-rate cash payment made to employees by their employer;

- to claim you must be both incapable of work and not actually do any work at all on the day in question;

- it is not payable for the first three agreed qualifying days in any period when you are too unwell to work; and

- in any period of sickness you have a maximum entitlement to 28 weeks of statutory sick pay.

(b) Statutory maternity pay

Eligibility for statutory maternity pay is again dependent on the payment of Class 1 contributions. A woman:

- qualifies for statutory maternity pay if she has been working continuously for the same employer for 26 weeks up to, and including, the 15th week before her baby is due;

- must provide evidence of being pregnant and give her employer sufficient notice of leaving work; and

- will receive benefit for 26 weeks beginning not earlier than the 11th week before the baby is due, although she can actually select the time over which she will be absent from work.

(c) Statutory paternity pay

The basic features of statutory paternity pay are:

- fathers are allowed up to two weeks away from work during the first eight weeks of their child's life;

- it is also a flat-rate cash payment; and

- the qualifying requirements are the same as those for statutory maternity pay.

(d) Jobseekers allowance

The key points of the jobseekers allowance, which is taxable, are:

- it is payable to unemployed individuals between the ages of 18 and state pension age who are available for work and are actively seeking employment;

- a claimant must sign a jobseekers agreement which sets out the steps he or she intends to take towards getting full-time employment;

- entitlement is based on either a satisfactory contribution record or a means-tested low income;

- it is a weekly benefit with supplements for age and other personal circumstances; and

- an individual is disqualified from receiving benefit if he or she fails to honour the obligations of the jobseekers agreement, or refuses to follow either recommendations or directions of the employment adviser.

(e) Incapacity benefit

Incapacity benefit is a contributory-based taxable benefit for individuals under state pension age who are unable to work because of illness or disability. Other key features are:

- employees normally get statutory sick pay for the first 28 weeks of sickness before they move on to incapacity benefit at the short-term higher rate;

- there are three different rates of benefit and additional supplements as well; and

- it is not means-tested.

(f) Income support

Income support is a non-contributory weekly benefit paid to individuals who do not have sufficient money to live on. The circumstances of each individual are looked at and their needs are assessed. Those with savings and capital over £16,000 do not qualify for income support.

(g) Child benefit

Child benefit is payable:

- to individuals bringing up children;

- for all children under 16 years old; and

- for children over age 16, but under 19, providing they are still in full-time education which includes courses at school or college up to 'A' level.

It is not means-tested and for couples who are married it is the mother who should make the claim.

(h) Benefits for the disabled

These include the disability living and attendance allowances. Disability living allowance:

- is a single benefit comprising two components – mobility and care; and

- can be paid for an indefinite period, but the first claim must be made before an individual's 65th birthday.

Attendance allowance is paid to people over 65 who are seriously disabled, mentally or physically, and who need a lot of care and attention.

(i) Benefits and rates

Listed in Appendix 6 at the end of the book are all the Social Security benefits, distinguishing between those which are taxable and non-taxable.

Following on is Appendix 7 which gives the rates of the main taxable Social Security benefits for 2006/07.

Pension Credit

An individual is entitled to the Pension Credit if he or she:

- lives in Great Britain;
- satisfies at least one of two requirements of the guarantee and savings credits respectively; and
- has reached the qualifying age.

The guarantee credit 'tops up' the income of a single claimant to £114.05 per week. For couples, including civil partners, the weekly income limit increases to £174.05. A claimant's income includes:

- a state and any other pension;
- earnings;
- Social Security benefits; and
- notional investment income of £1 a week for every £500 of savings or capital in excess of £6,000 (excluding your home and possessions).

The purpose of the savings credit, the rules for which are far from simple, is to reduce Pension Credit by 40% of the amount by which a pensioner's income exceeds the basic state pension.

The guarantee credit is available to both men and women who have reached age 60. The qualifying age for both men and women increases to age 65 for the savings credit.

9 STATE AND PRIVATE PENSIONS

I don't doubt that when you give up work and retire you will want to be able to maintain your lifestyle and living standards. You may have built up savings while you were working but your income in retirement is most likely to come from:

- the State Pension; and

- an employer or personal pension scheme.

So that you can give yourself the best possible opportunity to build up a good pension you should start contributing to a plan as soon as you can reasonably afford to do so.

State Pension

There are three parts to the state retirement pension:

- the basic retirement (or old person's) pension;

- a state-earnings-related pension (SERPS/S2P); and

- a graduated pension.

(a) Basic state pension

State pension age is the age at which you can claim your basic state pension. For men this is age 65 and, at the moment, age 60 for women.

To receive a full basic state pension you need:

- 44 qualifying years if you are a man; or

- 39 qualifying years if you are a woman.

A qualifying year is:

- Between April 1975 and April 1978, a tax year in which you earned at least 50 × the lower-earnings level for National Insurance purposes.

- Since April 1978, a tax year in which you have earned, or been credited with, earnings equivalent to at least 52 × the lower weekly earnings limit for National Insurance purposes.

You will not get any basic state pension if you retire with less than one-quarter of the qualifying years required for a full state pension.

(b) SERPS/S2P

As the name implies any entitlement to the state second pension depends on your earnings while you are working and the payment of Class 1 contributions.

The additional state pension, when it was first introduced in 1978, was known as SERPS. It was reformed in 2002 as S2P to provide a more generous additional state pension for individuals on low or moderate incomes.

(c) A graduated pension

You will have earned extra state pension if you paid graduated National Insurance contributions when the scheme was in operation between April 1961 and April 1975.

(d) Additional pension benefits

A man may receive extra pension for:

- a wife;
- dependent children; or
- a woman looking after his children.

A married woman receives a retirement pension either:

- by reference to her own contributions record; or
- based on her husband's contribution if she is over age 60 and retired, providing her husband is receiving the basic retirement pension; or
- as a wife dependent on her husband. He is then entitled to an increase in his pension.

The amount of retirement pension payable to a widow will depend upon whether she was widowed before or after the normal retirement age of 60.

Lump Sums

You can defer taking your State Pension and either:

- receive an increased pension when you actually take it; or
- be paid a lump sum.

If you opt for a simple addition to your future State Pension the higher weekly payment is the amount which is taxable when you start to receive it.

Under the lump sum alternative:

- The rate of pension is that fixed at the time you apply for deferral.

- The single payment will comprise both pension arrears, including increments, and interest thereon.

- The total amount is liable to income tax.

- It is not added to income for any tax purposes.

- The tax you pay on the lump sum is worked out by applying your marginal rate of tax.

- The Pension Service will deduct tax at source based on your declaration indicating your likely band of taxable income.

- You can elect for it to be paid and, therefore, taxed in the following tax year.

- You can do this at any time from the date you choose to receive the lump sum up to one month later.

- No further interest is added to the lump sum.

- The minimum deferral period is one of twelve consecutive months. There is no maximum length of time for which drawing your State Pension can be deferred.

- In most cases the Executors of a deceased persons Estate will be able to claim any undrawn lump sum benefit that had accrued up to the date of death.

Archie Barber is now in his late 60's. He was entitled to draw his State Pension in June 2005 but decided against doing so at the time. He chose to take his lump sum, amounting to £4,400, one year later in June 2006. In 2006/07 his total pension income amounted to £7,200 and he received gross interest on his building society account of £800, He only pays tax of £440 on his lump sum as follows:

	£
Pensions	7,200.00
Building Society interest	800.00
	8,000.00
Less: Personal age allowance	6,065.00
Taxable income	£1,935.00
2006/07 tax due: £1,935 × 10%	£193.50
Tax payable on lump sum State Pension: £4,400 × 10% (as a 10% tax payer)	£440.00

State Pension Forecast

You can get a state pension forecast if you are more than four months away from state pension age when your application is processed. Your forecast will advise you in today's money of the amounts of the three parts to the state retirement pension already earned. It will also tell you:

- what further state pension you might earn before you retire; and
- if there is anything you can do to improve your basic state pension.

The application form, BR19, can be obtained from the Pension Service by telephoning 0845 3000 168.

Private Pensions

There are a number of attractions in saving for your retirement through a private pension plan. If you are self-employed you will need to make your own arrangements. For those of you working in employment it is more than likely that your employer is running a scheme for the employees of the business which you can join.

The main features of pension provision are:

- You receive full tax relief on your premiums.

- Your contributions are invested in a tax-free fund.

- You can take your benefits at any time between the ages of 50 and 75.

- You do not have to retire to access your benefits.

- 25% of the value of your fund can be paid to you as a tax-free lump sum.

(a) Annual contributions

You can get tax relief on pension contributions up to 100% of your annual earnings, subject to a maximum annual allowance which is £215,000 for 2006/07. Non-earners and non-taxpayers can put up to £3,600 before tax each year into pension savings.

(b) Lifetime allowance

There is a single lifetime allowance on the amount of your pension savings that can benefit from tax relief. This limit was £1.5 million from April 2006 but it will go up each year. If the value of your pension fund is more than the lifetime allowance when you come to draw your pension you will be subject to tax on the excess.

(c) Transitional provisions

There are transitional arrangements to protect pension rights built up before 6 April 2006, including two options for transitional protection from the lifetime allowance tax charge.

(d) Death benefits

These can be in the form of:

- a lump sum;

- a pension for one or more dependents; or

- a combination of lump sum and pension.

10 SAVINGS AND INVESTMENT INCOME

There are likely to be occasions during your lifetime when you will either be:

- making regular savings out of income;

- investing a lump sum from a pension scheme on retirement; or

- in receipt of a much more substantial sum such as an inheritance or, perhaps, winnings on the National Lottery.

Examples of savings and investment income are bank or building society interest, share and unit trust dividends, rents, interest on government stocks and income from a trust fund.

Tax free income

The most widely known investments where the return is tax free are some of those available from National Savings and Investments. They are:

- Fixed-Interest and Index-Linked Savings Certificates;

- Children's Bonus Bonds; and

- Premium Bond Prizes.

Also tax free are:

- interest on your TESSA-ISA;

- income from your ISA and PEP investments; and

- dividends paid on your shares in Venture Capital Trusts.

Tax free income does not need to be reported on your annual Income Tax Return.

Interest and dividends

You will receive dividends on your shares or interest on your bank/ building society accounts or British Government stocks either:

- with a 10% tax credit which cannot be reclaimed;
- less Income Tax at 20%; or
- with no deduction for tax.

Non-repayable 10% tax credit	*Tax deducted at 20%*	*No tax deducted*
Dividends on shares	Bank and building society interest	National Savings:
Income distributions on unit trust holdings	National Savings Fixed Rate Savings Bonds	• Easy Access Savings Account
	*Interest on British Government Stocks with some exceptions	• Investment Account
		• Pensioners Bonds
	Income element of purchased life annuities	• Income and Capital Bonds
		*Interest on British Government Stocks
		Tax Deposit Certificates
		Single Deposits over £50,000 for a fixed period of less than five years
		Deposits with non-UK branches of banks and building societies

*Interest is always paid with no deduction for tax on the following holdings:

- 3.5% War Loan.
- Government Stocks held on the National Savings and Investments Register.

You can, if you want, choose to receive the interest on all other holdings of British Government stocks with no tax deducted. However, if the interest is being paid to you after deduction of tax and you would prefer to receive it with no tax deducted you will have to write to Computershare to request this change.

In working out how much tax you have to pay each year, dividend and interest income is always regarded as the top part of your income. If you have both dividend and interest (savings) income your dividends will be treated as the highest part. As a result:

- Non-taxpayers can only claim for a repayment of Income Tax on savings income where tax at 20% has been deducted before payment. The 10% tax credit on their dividend income is non-repayable.

Tanya Bridge, who is married to Derek, receives total investment income of £3,900 during 2006/07. £3,000 is the interest on her various building society accounts – £3,750 gross with tax of £750 (20%) taken off at source – and dividends of £900 (£1,000 gross less a 10% tax credit of £100).

Tanya's total income is less than her personal allowance of £5,035 but she can only claim back from HMRC the tax of £750 suffered on her interest income.

- Individuals liable to Income Tax at only the 10% starting rate are able to reclaim some of the tax at 20% deducted from their savings income.

Tanya's sister, Henrietta, earns £4,100 from part-time employment during 2006/07. All her savings are invested in cash deposits where she receives the interest with tax deducted and during the year it comes to £2,400. Her tax repayment for the year is £393.50 as follows:

	Gross income £	Tax incurred £
Employment earnings	4,100	–
Interest income	3,000	600.00
	7,100	600.00
Less: Personal allowance	5,035	
Taxable income	2,065	
Tax thereon: £2,065 at 10%		206.50
Repayment for 2006/07		£393.50

- Taxpayers liable at the basic rate of 22%, but not the top rate, do not pay any further tax on their dividend and interest income.

Tanya's aunt, Davina, receives building society interest, including tax deducted at source, of £1,200 in 2006/07. Her earned income, after allowances and reliefs, comes to £10,000. She pays tax for the year as follows:

on the first	£2,150 @ 10%
on the next	£7,850 @ 22%
on her interest income of	£1,200 @ 20%

- Individuals whose income takes them into the top tax rate of 40% must pay Income Tax of a further 20% on their non-dividend savings income above the basic-rate band. If the income beyond the basic-rate band comes from dividends the extra tax payable is at 32.5%.

Tanya's husband, Derek, banks interest and dividend income amounting to £6,800 (gross) and £2,600 (including the 10% tax credit) respectively during 2006/07. His earnings, after allowances and reliefs, total £27,000. His tax charge is worked out as follows:

on the first	£2,150 @ 10%
on the next	£24,850 @ 22%
on his interest income of	£6,300 @ 20%
on his interest income of	£500 @ 40%
on his dividends	£2,600 @ 32.5%

The £6,300 slice of interest income attracts tax at the rate of 20% as it falls within the limit of income of £31,150 taxed at the basic rate.

Individuals not liable to tax can arrange to receive their interest gross. This is done by completing special forms which are available at banks, building societies, post offices and tax offices throughout the country as well as from the HMRC website.

Accrued income

Interest on fixed-rate investments is regarded as accruing from day-to-day between payment dates. On a sale the vendor is charged Income Tax on the interest that has accrued from the previous payment date to the date of sale. The purchaser is allowed to deduct this amount from the interest received on the following payment date.

These arrangements cover both fixed and variable-rate stocks and bonds, including those issued by Governments, companies and local authorities. But the arrangements will not affect you if the nominal value of your securities is under £5,000.

> The interest on a holding of 8% Treasury Stock 2013 is payable on each 27 March and 27 September. The half-yearly interest on a holding of £20,000, sold for settlement on 14 July 2006, is £1,000.
>
> $$\text{Accrued proportion} = \frac{109}{183} \times £1,000 = £595.63$$

Rents

The letting of property, including isolated or casual lettings, is treated as a business for tax purposes. This applies to any flat, house, shop or other property that you rent to tenants. Most of the rules for working out the taxable profits from a trade or profession are also relevant in working out your annual income from the letting of property. Income from all your properties in the UK is pooled together, regardless of the type of lease. Also it does not matter whether the property is let furnished or unfurnished.

However, unlike a trade or profession, losses from your property rental business can only be carried forward to be set against future profits from the same activities.

Other than expenditure of a capital nature, such as that on extensions, structural alterations or improvements, the general running costs of a property can be set against rental income. Included in allowable expenses are:

- fees incurred on letting out the property, including estate agents' costs, advertisements and the fees for drawing up an inventory;

- rent collection and management costs;
- interest relating to your property letting business. It does not matter whether the interest is payable on a loan or overdraft;
- maintenance, repairs and redecorations;
- insurance premiums on buildings and contents policies;
- rents and water rates;
- council tax paid for your tenants;
- gardening, cleaning and security services;
- all other expenses of managing the property such as stationery, postage, advertising for tenants etc; and
- your share of expenditure on the common parts of the let property.

If you improve the energy use of a residential property which you let out you can claim a deduction against your rents for expenditure of up to £1,500 spent on each property for:

- loft or wall insulation;
- draught proofing; and/or
- insulating the hot water system.

These costs would normally be treated as improvements. As such they could not be offset against rental income without this special tax relief.

Karen Donnelly owns a flat which she let out to tenants during 2006/07. The net rental income for the year amounts to £14,740 as follows:

		£	£
Rent receivable from the flat			21,000
Less:	Expenses		
	Agents fees for letting	2,467	
	Management fees	740	
	Ground rent	200	
	Service charges	1,103	
	Council tax for tenants	960	
	Water rates	220	
	Lounge redecoration	490	
	Boiler repair	80	
			6,260
2006/07 net rental income			£14,740

Where you are renting out:

- Unfurnished property, you can claim capital allowances on the cost of fixtures, fittings and equipment spent on the let property.

- Furnished property, you are allowed an additional deduction to cover the cost of wear and tear to furnishings and fittings which can be what you actually spend on renewing them. Alternatively you can claim a fixed allowance equivalent to 10% of the rent you receive less amounts paid out on Council Tax and water rates.

If Karen's flat in the preceding illustration had been let furnished this allowance would amount to £1,982 as follows:

	£
Rent receivable	21,000
Less: Council Tax and water rates	1,180
	£19,820
Wear and tear allowance: 10%	£1,982

The rules dealing with the taxation of premiums on leases are more complicated and outside the scope of this book.

Rent-a-Room

Income from the furnished letting of spare rooms in your home is tax free providing the gross rents do not exceed £4,250 per annum. The space you let out must be in your only or main home which can be a house, flat, caravan or even a houseboat.

You can elect to opt out of this special form of relief. It will pay you to make the opt-out election if, for example, there is a loss on the letting which can be set against your other rental profits under the normal rules dealing with income from lettings.

Where your annual gross rents are more than £4,250 you must elect if you want to pay tax on the excess gross rents, without any relief for expenses. If you do not do so then you will have to work out your taxable income using the rules for lettings income.

Theresa Stevens is a basic-rate taxpayer who lets out a room in her bungalow to a lodger paying £110 per week, £5,720 for 2006/07. The expenses that could be set against the lodgers rents total £1,600 for the year.

Theresa elects for Rent-a-Room relief and her Income Tax liability is £323.40 – (£5,720 - £4,250) x 22%. Under the normal rules her tax liability would come to £906.40 – (£5,720 – £1,600) x 22%.

The tax free limit of £4,250 is halved where an individual and some other person are each entitled to income under the scheme. Each lessor's exempt amount is then £2,125.

Non-qualifying life policies

At the outset, a lump sum premium is paid into a Bond which is, for example, either investment based or intended to produce a guaranteed income. An investor can usually:

- take regular amounts out;
- make ad hoc partial withdrawals; or
- leave the Bond untouched until encashment or death when it will form part of the investor's estate.

There is no tax relief on the single premium. Neither Capital Gains Tax nor Income Tax at the savings rate is payable on any profit. But investors whose income takes them into the top rate of 40% will pay tax at the difference between the higher and savings rates of Income Tax on chargeable events. These arise on:

- surrender or maturity of the policy;
- death of the life assured; or
- withdrawals in excess of a cumulative allowance built up at the time.

At the end of each policy year an allowance of 5% of the original investment is given. This can be carried forward from year to year. Over a period of 20 years, allowances of up to 100% of the initial investment will be given. A taxable gain only arises if the amount of the withdrawal is more than the cumulative allowance at the time. Then it is the excess which is taxed.

Edward Clark invests £15,000 in an Investment Bond. Withdrawals of £600, £900 and £3,250 are made during the second, third and fifth policy years. The annual allowance is £750 being 5%, of the original investment. A taxable gain of £1,000 arises in year five as follows:

Number of Policy Years	Cumulative Allowance	Amount Withdrawn	Cumulative Withdrawals	Taxable Amount
	£	£	£	£
1	750	—	—	—
2	1,500	600	600	—
3	2,250	900	1,500	—
4	3,000	—	1,500	—
5	3,750	3,250	4,750	1,000

When the final chargeable event on a Bond occurs, the taxable gain is calculated by taking into account all previous withdrawals and taxable gains.

After seven years, Edward encashes the Investment Bond in the illustration above for £21,050. The taxable gain amounts to £9,800 as follows:

	£	£
Policy proceeds		21,050
Add: Withdrawals in years 2, 3 and 5		4,750
		25,800
Less: Original investment	15,000	
Amount already taxed	1,000	
		16,000
Taxable gain on encashment		£9,800

The method of calculating the Income Tax due on the taxable gain involves a number of stages, including 'top slicing' relief.

Edward, is a single man. During 2006/07 his other income, all earnings, amounted to £37,545. He pays tax of £853.48 on the gain of £9,800 on the final encashment of his Bond worked out as follows:

Gain on encashment of Bond	£9,800
Number of years held	7
Taxable slice of gain	£1,400
Taxable income – excluding slice of gain	
Earnings	37,545
Less: Personal allowance	5,035
	£32,510
Tax applicable to slice of gain	
On first £790 (£33,300 – £32,510) @ 0%	—
On next £610 (excess over £33,300)	
20% (40% – 20%)	£122.00
Average rate on slice	8.71%
The tax payable on the gain =	
£9,800 @ 8.71% =	£853.58

Individual Savings Accounts

An Individual Savings Account (ISA) can include up to two components:

- cash (including National Savings); and

- stocks and shares.

You can subscribe to an ISA if you are:

- both resident and ordinarily resident in the UK for tax purposes; and

- aged 18 or over, although 16- and 17-year-olds can invest in just the cash component.

The annual subscription limit is £7,000 of which no more than £3,000 can go into cash. Other features of an ISA are:

- The account is completely free of tax.

- There is no statutory lock-in period or minimum subscription. You can make withdrawals whenever you like.

- There is no lifetime investment limit.

The list of investments which qualify for the stocks and shares component include:

- shares listed on a recognized Stock Exchange;

- Unit Trusts;

- Investment Trusts;

- Open-ended investment companies; and

- Government stocks with at least five years to go to maturity.

Each year savers have two choices when it comes to appointing their plan managers. The first option allows them to go to a single manager who must offer an account that can accept the overall subscription. This means that:

- the account must include the stocks and shares component, but does not need to offer cash;

- savers can subscribe up to £7,000 for stocks and shares; and

- if, in addition, the plan manager offers the cash component, savers can deposit up to £3,000 in cash, and the balance of £4,000 can go into stocks and shares.

Under the second option savers can go to separate managers – one for each component – and subscribe:

- up to £4,000 in stocks and shares; and

- £3,000 to cash.

These fixed individual limits have been designed to ensure that the overall annual investment limit can be satisfactorily monitored.

TESSA-ISA

A Tax-Exempt Special Savings Account (TESSA) was a savings scheme with a bank, building society or other institution where the interest earned was tax free. No new TESSA could be taken out after ISAs were introduced. However, existing TESSAs were allowed to run their full five-year course.

When a TESSA matured, savers could transfer their capital, but not the accumulated interest, into the cash component of an ISA. Such a transfer did not affect the amount that could be subscribed to an ISA. So long as the account remains in being the interest is tax free.

Personal Equity Plans

Personal Equity Plans (PEPs) are an ongoing way of investing in shares. However, after the introduction of ISAs no new money could be invested in PEPs. But existing PEPs held then can continue with the following benefits:

- they are free of tax;

- there are no tax penalties on withdrawing from or closing down a plan; and

- the investments that can be held in the plan are the same as those which are allowed for the stocks and shares component of an ISA.

Enterprise Investment Scheme

The aims of the Scheme are twofold:

- To provide a targeted incentive for equity investment in unquoted trading companies which help overcome the problems faced by such companies in raising modest amounts of equity finance.

- To encourage outside investors previously unconnected with the company, who introduce finance and expertise, by allowing them actively to participate in the management of the company as paid directors without losing entitlement to relief.

The main features of the Scheme are:

- Income Tax relief at 20% on qualifying investments up to £400,000 in any tax year;

- Income Tax relief on up to one-half of the amount invested between 6 April and 5 October in a tax year can be carried back to the previous tax year, subject to a maximum limit of £50,000;

- all shares in a qualifying company must be held for at least three years; otherwise the Income Tax relief will be clawed back; and

- losses made on the disposal of qualifying shares are eligible for relief from either Income Tax or Capital Gains Tax.

Venture Capital Trusts

Venture Capital Trusts (VCTs) are a type of Investment Trust with tax advantages designed to encourage investment in the under-nourished small-business sector. Individuals investing in VCTs are eligible for the following Income Tax incentives:

- relief at 30% on subscriptions for new ordinary shares up to £200,000 in any tax year, providing the shares are held for at least five years; and

- tax free dividends.

Overseas investment income

Generally, income from investments or savings abroad is taxed in the same way as your onshore dividends or interest income. Foreign tax paid, subject to certain restrictions, can be offset against the tax payable here on the same income. If required, you must be able to show that you have actually paid, or suffered, the overseas tax.

Joint income

Income from assets such as bank/building society accounts, property or shares held in the joint names of a married couple or civil partners is treated for tax purposes as belonging to them in equal proportions. If the actual proportions of ownership between the couple are unequal they can make an election for the income on any jointly owned assets to be taxed in accordance with their respective entitlements to the income. There is a special form to complete. The declaration applies from the date it is made.

But dividends from jointly owned shares in a small family company are taxed on husband and wife according to their actual ownership, rather than in equal shares.

11 THE FAMILY UNIT

Gone are the days when it was common place for couples to marry. Many now prefer to live together as partners. Opposite sex couples may even have children without marrying or marry later on in life.

Living together

There are no special tax breaks for couples living with one another as partners. They are each taxed as single people. Furthermore, it is mandatory that income from jointly owned assets must be split between them in accordance with the ratio of their respective interests in such assets. Assets cannot be transferred between them without avoiding a possible liability to Capital Gains Tax at the time of transfer.

Marriage

Husband and wife:

- are taxed separately on their income and capital gains;

- are each entitled to personal allowances which can be set against their own income, whether from earnings or investments;

- can each have taxable income, after allowances and reliefs of £33,300 for 2006/07 before either of them is liable to tax at the top rate of 40%. They may, of course, need to rearrange their affairs to take maximum advantage of potential tax savings. In contrast to the position of unmarried couples this is easily done;

- must complete their own Tax Returns every year; and

- are each responsible for settling their respective tax liabilities.

These rules also apply to same-sex couples who have legalized their relationship by forming a Civil Partnership.

Children

A child is:

- treated as an individual for tax purposes like anyone else;
- entitled to the personal allowance, so no tax is probably payable on any earnings from, for example, a daily paper round;
- also a taxable person for the purposes of Capital Gains Tax (Chapter 13) and Inheritance Tax (Chapter 17).

But, the income from a gift by a parent in favour of an unmarried minor child is regarded as the parents' income for tax purposes – subject to an annual £100 limit for small amounts of income. Grandparents or other relatives can, however, give savings to their grandchildren or nieces, nephews, etc, without the same restrictions applying to the taxation of income on any such gifts.

Savers such as children, who are not taxpayers, can elect to receive gross interest on their bank or building society accounts. As an alternative to this type of investment for your child's savings, why not take a look at the Children's Bonus Bonds issued by National Savings and Investments which are particularly suitable for investing gifts from parents. The return on these Bonds is exempt from both Income Tax and Capital Gains Tax.

There is no general tax allowance for children. However:

- you should be able to claim Child Benefit and may be due Child Tax Credit (see Chapter 3); or
- depending on your personal circumstances you may be entitled to one or more of the numerous other Social Security benefits associated with children.

It is down to parents or guardians to complete and sign Tax Returns or Repayment Claims for their children up to age 18.

The Child Trust Fund

The Child Trust Fund (CTF) is a savings and investment plan for children, the main features of which are:

- a child receives a voucher from the Government for a lump sum of £250 shortly after birth;

- eligibility is dependent on the parent making a claim for child benefit. Children from low-income families receive an additional £250;

- the Government will make a further payment of £250 when a child reaches age seven. At the same age children from lower-income families will receive £500;

- up to £1,200 each year can be added to the fund by family and friends;

- all income and capital growth within a CTF is tax free; and

- it can be accessed at age 18.

Within 12 months of issue a parent must use the voucher to open a CTF account for the child. There are a wide range of organizations offering CTF accounts linked to either cash deposits, unit trusts or even equities.

Separation and divorce

Not only does the breakdown of a marriage cause much personal suffering but it invariably has consequences for tax purposes.

A married couple are no longer considered to be living together when:

- they are separated by a Deed or Court Order; or

- they are living apart in such a way that permanent separation is inevitable.

If a married couple are entitled to the married couple's allowance, the full allowance can be claimed by the husband for the tax year in which the marriage fails, but if he remarries in the same year he cannot also claim that part of the allowance due for the period following the wedding.

Maintenance payments are tax free in the hands of the recipient, but only limited tax relief is available to the payer of maintenance under a Court Order, Child Support Agency assessment or written agreement as follows:

- either the payer or recipient must be born before 6 April 1935;

- the payment must be to the divorced or separated spouse;

- the maximum amount of tax relief to which the payer is entitled is 10% of the lesser of £2,350 or the actual maintenance paid each year; and

- no tax relief can be claimed on maintenance paid to, or for the benefit of, children of the marriage.

The tax implications for civil partners who separate are no different to those for a married couple. Similarly the dissolution of a Civil Partnership has the same consequences as a divorce of an opposite sex couple.

Old age

When it comes to tax, getting older does not mean an easier life. Pensioners have to deal with the tax system in the same way as everyone else. Nevertheless, there are some factors which are only relevant to:

- the finances of elderly persons; and
- working out how much tax they must pay each year.

First and foremost come the age allowances. In Chapter 2, I explained how a pensioner calculates the amount of these allowances to which he or she is entitled.

Men qualify to receive the State Pension when they reach age 65; for women it is currently age 60. The State Pension includes:

- the basic retirement (or old person's) pension;
- a state earnings-related pension (SERPS/S2P);
- a graduated pension; and
- the age addition if you are over 80.

On reaching retirement age a pensioner has three options:

- retire and claim the state pension;
- carry on working and claim the state pension; or
- put off taking the state pension.

If you choose to defer taking your state pension you can claim:

- additional state pension when you eventually retire; or
- a lump sum – equal to the state pension to which you would have been entitled during the period of deferment, plus compound interest.

All pensions, including a State Pension, are taxable. There is, however, no mechanism to deduct any Income Tax at source from payment of the State Pension. Therefore, in addition to including a pensioner's personal allowance in the coding notice of an occupational or personal pension taxed under PAYE, it also incorporates a deduction from allowances equivalent to the annual amount of the State Pension. In this way:

- the tax due on the State Pension is collected; and

- the need to make a direct tax payment is avoided.

The significance of the following letters at the end of a Code Number is as follows:

- V – indicates the pensioner is entitled to both the personal and married couple's allowances for ages 65–74 and pays tax at the basic rate.

- P – indicates the full personal allowance is due for those aged 65–74.

- Y – means you are due the full personal allowance for age 75 and over.

- T – applies in most other circumstances.

If a pensioner's State Pension exceeds his or her personal allowance, HMRC issue a 'K' Coding. The amount of the negative allowance is then added to the pension on which tax is paid.

Taxpayers approaching State Pension age should make sure that their Notice of Coding is changed to include an estimate of the amount of their State Pension for the year. Usually HMRC sends such taxpayers a Form P161 asking for details about pension entitlement. This information is then used to amend tax codes as appropriate.

Nowadays many people carry on working after they retire from their main job or self-employment. They may decide to make use of all the knowledge and experience built up during their working lives by setting up in business as a consultant, or take a part-time position in, for example, a retail outlet.

Owen Wilcox is single and 68. During 2006/07 he received a State Pension of £86.15 per week and an annual pension from his previous employer of £6,000. To keep himself occupied he worked part-time at his local DIY Store earning a weekly wage of £105 for 46 weeks of the year. Owen paid Income Tax for 2006/07 of £1,508.60 as follows:

	Income	Tax
	£	£
State Pension	4,480	
Occupational Pension	6,000	446.00
Wages	4,830	1,062.60
	15,310	£1,508.60

Less: Personal Allowance	7,280	
Taxable Income	£8,030	
Income Tax payable		
£2,150 @ 10%		215.00
£5,880 @ 22%		1,293.60
		£1,508.60

The tax code used for working out the Income Tax to be deducted from Owen's occupational pension is 280P. This is based on the difference between Owen's personal age allowance of £7,280 and his State Pension of £4,480. Tax at the basic rate of 22%, under a BR Code, would have been deducted from Owen's wage from the DIY store.

To gain maximum advantage from the personal age and married couple's allowance, as well as paying tax at the 10% rate on the full amount of income in the starting rate band – £2,150 for 2006/07 – elderly married couples with modest incomes may need to transfer capital between themselves.

Bert and Mavis Wilkins, a married couple, both in their early 70s, whose joint income for 2006/07 amounted to £42,000, paid Income Tax of £5,511.30 on this sum. This mainly related to Bert's income as follows:

	Bert	*Mavis*
	£	£
State Pensions	4,381	2,626
Occupational Pensions	12,619	3,284
Building Society Interest		
Gross equivalent	11,000	1,890
Interest on British Government Stocks	5,000	1,200
	33,000	9,000
Less: Personal Allowance	5,035	7,280
Taxable Income	£27,965	£1,720

Income Tax Payable

£2,150/£1,720 @ 10%	215.00	172.00
£9,815 @ 22%	2,159.30	—
£16,000 @ 20% (savings income)	3,200.00	—
	5,574.30	172.00
Less: Relief for married couple's allowance – £2,350 @ 10%	235.00	—
	£5,339.30	£172.00

Bert's income is above the upper limit for entitlement to either personal age or married couple's allowances, whereas Mavis has insufficient income to benefit from the full starting-rate tax band of £2,150.

Significant tax savings of £699.40 for 2006/07 could have been achieved by the couple if Bert had transferred capital to Mavis as follows:

	Bert	Mavis
	£	£
State Pensions	4,381	2,626
Occupational Pensions	12,619	3,284
Building Society Interest Gross equivalent	3,600	9,290
Interest on British Government Stocks	1,400	4,800
	22,000	20,000
Less: Personal Allowance	6,330	7,280
Taxable Income	£15,670	£12,720
Income Tax payable		
£2,150/£2,150 @ 10%	215.00	215.00
£8,520 @ 22%	1,874.40	—
£5,000/£10,570 @ 20% (savings income)	1,000.00	2,114.00
	3,089.40	2,329.00

Less: Relief for married couple's allowance – £6,065 @ 10%	606.50	—
	£2,482.90	£2,329.00

Death

Sadly, death comes to all of us and has tax consequences for married couples which are:

- the married couple's allowance is not restricted in the year of death of either spouse;

- where the husband dies first, he is due his full personal allowance in the year of death. If he cannot use up the full married couple's allowance, because he has a low income, then the balance can be transferred to his widow; or

- if the wife dies before her husband she will be due her full personal allowance in the year of death.

Civil partners are treated no differently.

12   THE OVERSEAS ELEMENT

Apart from some special cases, the amount of tax you pay each year depends on whether you are resident in the United Kingdom (UK) and, to a lesser extent, on your domicile status. If you live permanently in the UK then, generally, all your income arising in this country will be liable to UK taxation. Overseas income is similarly taxable although special rules apply in taxing foreign income of individuals resident, but not domiciled, in the UK.

Not only are the two concepts of domicile and residence of fundamental importance in determining the extent of an individual's liability to UK taxation on income, they are of equal significance for the purposes of both Capital Gains Tax and Inheritance Tax.

Domicile

Your domicile will generally be considered to be the country or state which you regard as your permanent homeland. Your domicile is separate from your residence or nationality. When you are born you acquire a domicile of origin from your father. You can abandon your original domicile by birth if you settle in another country or state with a view to making it your new permanent home. Provided you sever all links with your current country of domicile you can move towards acquiring a domicile of choice in the new country. You should be prepared to provide a substantial amount of evidence that you propose to live there for ever.

A wife's domicile is not necessarily the same as her husband's domicile if they were married at some time after the end of 1973. It is decided by the same factors as for any other individual who is able to have an independent domicile. A woman who married before the beginning of 1974 automatically acquired the domicile of her husband on marriage. So long as the marriage lasts, her domicile only alters when there is any change in the domicile of her husband.

If you think you have good grounds for believing that you should not be regarded as domiciled in the UK you should write to your Tax Office about this. Usually, you can then expect to receive a questionnaire which you should fill in and send back to your Tax Office. The information you have supplied will be considered by the HMRC Specialist Department that deals with these matters. In due course you will receive a ruling on your domicile status.

Residence and ordinary residence

There is no statutory definition of residence and ordinary residence. Each case must be judged on the facts. What follows is a summary of the main factors that will be taken into account.

Without exception you will always be regarded as resident in the UK if you spend 183 days or more here in the tax year. Days of arrival in, and departure from, the UK are normally left out of account in working out the number of days spent here.

If you are here for less than 183 days you will still be treated as resident where you visit the UK regularly and after four tax years your visits during those years average 91 days or more in a tax year. From the fifth year you are treated as a UK resident.

You are also regarded as ordinarily resident in the UK if you are resident here from year to year. It is possible to be resident, but not ordinarily resident. For example, you may normally live outside the UK but are in this country for at least 183 days in a tax year. Conversely you can occasionally be considered to be ordinarily resident, but not actually resident, for a particular tax year. This could happen if you live in the UK but, for some reason, are abroad for a complete tax year.

Calculating annual average visits

The set formula to be used in working out the average number of days spent in the UK each year is:

$$\frac{\text{total visits to the UK (in days)}}{\text{total period since leaving (in days)}} \times 365 \text{ days} = \text{annual average visits}$$

The maximum period over which the average is taken is four years.

Thomas Winter, a retired solicitor, left the UK on 23 November 2003. In the period from the date of his departure to 5 April 2004 he visited the UK for 43 days. In the following three tax years to 5 April 2007, he spent 110, 85 and 57 days in the UK. The average number of days in the UK works out at 87.61 as follows:

$$\frac{43 + 110 + 85 + 57}{133 + 365 + 366 + 365} = \frac{295}{1,229} \times 365 = 87.61 \text{ days}$$

As this is less than the 91 days per annum average Thomas will be treated as non-resident throughout the period.

Working abroad – long absences

Poor job prospects in the UK, together with higher salaries and low taxation abroad, may prompt you to look for work overseas. This is likely to involve living abroad permanently for a time. Your probable residence status is clearly set out in paragraphs 2:2 and 2:3 of the HMRC booklet IR20 – *Residents and Non-Residents* – as follows:

'If you leave the UK to work full time abroad under a contract of employment, you are treated as not resident and not ordinarily resident if you meet all the following conditions:

- your absence from the UK and your employment abroad both last for at least a whole tax year;

- during your absence any visits you make to the UK:

    — total less than 183 days in any tax year, and

    — average less than 91 days a tax year (the average is taken over the period of absence up to a maximum of four years; any dates spent in the UK because of exceptional circumstances beyond your control, for example the illness of yourself or a member of your immediate family, are not normally counted for this purpose).

Should you meet all of the above conditions you are treated as not resident and not ordinarily resident in the UK from the day after you leave the UK to the date before you return to the UK at the end of your employment abroad. You are treated as coming to the UK permanently on the day you return from your employment abroad and as resident and ordinarily resident from that date.'

There will be no tax to pay here on your salary for the part of the tax year after you have left the UK.

There is no specific definition of when employment abroad is 'full-time'. Each particular case must be considered on all the facts. Nevertheless, where your employment involves a standard pattern of hours, it will be regarded as full time if your working hours each week are comparable with those that would be worked in the UK. Furthermore, several part-time jobs all at the same time could be taken as constituting full-time employment.

If you leave the UK to work full time in a trade, profession or vocation overseas and fulfil the same conditions as anyone taking up full-time employment abroad then your UK residence status will be determined in the same way.

You may well take your spouse with you. By concession he or she may also be regarded as neither resident nor ordinarily resident for the same period even if your spouse does not work abroad.

Working abroad – expenses

Tax relief is allowed on travel expenses you incur in relation to your overseas employment. Nor will you be taxed on the cost of board and lodging provided for you where the expenses are borne by your employer.

Generally, whenever your job takes you overseas, even for short periods, you will not be taxed on the cost of your travelling expenses so long as your employer meets the bills. This also applies to the costs of unlimited return visits to the UK during longer assignments abroad.

No taxable benefit arises where your employer meets the travelling costs of your spouse and children to visit you overseas. Not more than two return visits by the same person are allowed each year, and you must be working abroad for a continuous period of at least 60 days.

Leaving the UK permanently

Where you go abroad to live permanently, or to live outside the UK for three years or more, you will provisionally be considered neither resident nor ordinarily resident in the UK from the day following your departure. You should be prepared to provide sufficient evidence of your intention to make a permanent home somewhere outside the UK. Provided you do not infringe the rules about visits to the UK the provisional non-resident ruling will subsequently be confirmed by HMRC. You are entitled to full allowances and reliefs for the year of departure.

Before you leave, ask your Tax Office for the special form (P85) to be completed by individuals going abroad. The information in the form about your intended residence position will enable HMRC to make an in-year tax refund to you if, for example, you are claiming split-year treatment.

When you become not ordinarily resident in the UK you can apply to receive interest on any bank or building society account here without deduction of tax. Similarly, Income Tax is not charged on the interest from certain UK Government securities.

Allowances for non-UK residents

You may be able to claim UK tax allowances if you are not resident here. If you are eligible to claim you will generally be entitled to the same allowances as an individual resident in the UK. The following individuals can claim:

- a citizen of the Commonwealth;
- a citizen of a state within the European Union;
- a present or former employee of the British Crown;
- a resident of the Isle of Man or the Channel Islands; and
- certain other specific classes of individuals.

Income from UK property

Many individuals choose to rent out their homes while they are away, particularly when they go to work abroad. You can apply to HMRC for a certificate authorizing your tenant, or managing agent, to make payments of rent to you without deducting UK tax. If no such certificate is issued, tax at the basic rate must be withheld from all remittances of rent to you.

Even though you are not resident in the UK you could still be liable to UK tax on income arising from the letting out of UK property. This is so whether or not tax is deducted by your tenant or letting agent.

However, you will not actually have any UK tax to pay if your total income, including your income from property after allowable expenses, chargeable to UK tax, is less than any allowances which you may be entitled to claim.

Double taxation relief

If you move to a country with which the UK has concluded a Double Taxation Agreement, you may be able to claim partial or full exemption from UK tax on certain types of income from UK sources. Normally, you should be entitled to some measure of relief from UK tax on pensions and annuities, royalties and dividends. Many Double Taxation Agreements contain clauses dealing with the special circumstances of teachers and researchers, students and apprentices, and entertainers and sportsmen/women.

Going abroad – Capital Gains Tax

If you have been resident in the UK for at least four out of the last seven years ending with the day you leave and, within five years, you return here to take up residence for tax purposes again, then the concessionary split-year tax treatment does not apply for the purposes of Capital Gains Tax. You will be classified as a UK resident for the entire tax years of both departure and return.

It follows that gains realized in the tax year of departure will be taxed in that year. All gains in subsequent years, including the year of return, will be subject to Capital Gains Tax in the year when residence resumes. Profits made on assets bought and sold during the years of non-UK tax residence will not, however, be liable to Capital Gains Tax in the UK.

Taking up UK residence

Perhaps you have been working overseas, your contract has come to an end and you are thinking about returning here. Before you take up UK residence again there are some specific tax-planning points which must be considered. For example, any bank deposit or building society accounts should be closed before you return as you could otherwise face the prospect of a charge to UK Income Tax on interest accrued, but not credited, during your period of non-residence.

If the UK is not your normal homeland you should initially be able to satisfy HMRC that you have an overseas domicile. Any income from investments here is taxable as it arises. Your overseas investment income is not taxed unless it is actually remitted or enjoyed here. Where your job is with either a UK or an overseas employer, and the duties of your employment are performed wholly in the UK, the full amount of your salary is taxable here. Appendix 8 at the end of the book is a summary of the scope of liability to Income Tax of earnings.

You will be treated as resident and ordinarily resident from the date you arrive if you are either coming here permanently or intending to stay for at least three years. You will be able to claim full UK personal allowances for the year of arrival.

You should let HMRC know when you come to the UK. You will normally be asked to complete a Form P86 which will help to determine your residence status. The form also includes a section on domicile so that it will be possible, in straightforward cases, to deal with both your residence status and domicile together. This will apply, for example, if you:

- have never been domiciled within the UK;

- have come here only to work; and

- intend to leave the UK once your employment ceases.

13   CAPITAL GAINS

The profits you make on disposing of your assets are known as capital gains and are subject to Capital Gains Tax. However, not all capital receipts are taxable. These include lottery, pools or gambling winnings, mortgage cash-backs and personal or professional damages. Profits made on disposing of the following types of asset are also tax free:

- private cars;

- National Savings;

- your home;

- chattels sold for less than £6,000;

- British Government securities and many corporate bonds;

- shares issued under the Enterprise Investment Scheme as long as the income tax relief has not been withdrawn;

- shares in Venture Capital Trusts;

- investments in a Personal Equity Plan (PEP) or Individual Savings Account (ISA);

- gifts to charities or for the public benefit; and

- qualifying life policies on your life.

Taxable gains

This list includes profits you realize from disposing of:

- property;

- shares and unit trust investments;

- chattels sold for more than £6,000; and

- foreign currency other than that for personal use.

For Capital Gains Tax purposes, the date when the contract for purchase or sale is made determines the date when an asset is acquired or sold.

Tax payable

Every tax year you can make gains up to the annual exemption limit without paying tax. For 2006/07 the tax-free allowance is £8,800. The tax on gains over and above this limit is worked out by adding the excess to your taxable income.

Michael Garner made chargeable gains of £14,400 from selling shares in 2006/07. His taxable income from all sources, after personal allowances and other reliefs, was £28,200. The Capital Gains Tax he owes for 2006/07 is £1,220 as follows:

	£
Chargeable gains	14,400
Less: Annual exemption	8,800
	5,600
Tax payable	
£5,100 @ 20% (Savings Rate)	1,020
£500 @ 40%	200
2006/07 Capital Gains Tax payable	£1,220

The amount of Capital Gains Tax at 20% is worked out on the difference between the £33,300 limit of income taxable at the starting and basic rates and Michael's income of £28,200.

Any allowances or reliefs that you are unable to use because your income is too low cannot be set against your capital gains.

Husband and wife

Husband and wife are:

• separately entitled to the annual exemption limit; and

- individually taxed on chargeable gains they realize in a tax year in excess of the annual exemption limit.

A married couple living together can transfer assets between them without gain or loss as follows:

- the recipient spouse is deemed to have acquired such assets at the cost to the former spouse;

- the transferee spouse does not inherit the status (business or non-business) that the asset had when owned by the transferor spouse;

- this exemption ceases when a couple permanently separate.

It is not uncommon for a married couple to own assets in their joint names. For tax purposes, a profit on disposal of a jointly owned asset is apportioned between husband and wife in the ratio of their respective interests in that asset at the date of disposal.

These rules extend to civil partners.

Working out chargeable gains

In calculating the taxable gain on the disposal of a chargeable asset, you are allowed to make certain deductions from the proceeds of sale as follows:

- the purchase price;

- incidental costs incurred on acquiring the asset;

- any additional expenditure you have incurred on enhancing the value of the asset, such as improvements or alterations to a property, during your period of ownership; and

- the costs of sale.

The list of incidental expenses which are allowed as either purchase or sale costs includes:

- solicitor's fees, including transfer and conveyancing costs;

- surveyor's, valuer's or auctioneer's fees;

- broker's commission;

- estate agent's commission, including advertising expenses;

- Stamp Duty Land Tax; and

- valuation costs.

In the following sections in this chapter, you will read about the indexation allowance and taper relief, both of which may be applied to the mathematical profit on sale in arriving at the amount of the chargeable gain on which you pay tax.

Relief for losses

Losses and gains made in the same tax year are offset against each other. Any excess losses can be carried forward, without time limit, to reduce gains in subsequent tax years. But losses can never reduce the amount of your gains to below the annual exemption limit.

Bernard Levy had unused capital losses of £8,100 at 5 April 2006. During 2006/07 he made gains of £23,700 and incurred losses of £10,800.

His capital gains position for the year is:

	£	£
Gains realized in the year		23,700
Less: Losses — in the year	10,800	
— brought forward (part)	4,100	
		14,900
2006/07 Exemption limit		£8,800

The unused losses at 5 April 2007 of £4,000 can be carried forward to be set against gains in later years.

A loss:

- Arising on the sale or gift of an asset to a person with whom you are connected can only be set off against a gain on a similar disposal at a later date.

- Can be claimed where the value of an asset you own becomes negligible or nil. You do not actually have to dispose of the asset. The loss arises on the date that the relief is claimed. In practice, however, a two-year period is allowed from the end of the tax year in which the asset became of negligible value.

- On shares you subscribe for in a trading company not quoted on a recognized stock exchange can be set against your income, rather than against other capital gains. This applies whether you realize a loss on disposing of such shares or they become worthless.

The indexation allowance

This allowance, which ceased from April 1998, increases the cost of an asset and any enhancement expenditure by inflation. The allowance is calculated as follows:

- It is determined by the movement in the Retail Prices Index in the period of ownership up to April 1998. For assets that you possessed before April 1982, the starting date for calculating this allowance is March 1982.

- When you dispose of an asset that you acquired before 6 April 1982, the allowance can be calculated on either the market value of the asset at 31 March 1982 or its actual cost, whichever is greater. Where you have elected for capital gains on all disposals of assets you owned on 31 March 1982 to be worked out on their values at that date, ignoring original costs, the allowance can only be calculated on those values.

- No allowance can be claimed where an asset is sold at a loss. Neither can the indexation allowance turn a gain into a loss. It can only reduce a gain to nil.

The indexation allowance for April 1998 is in Appendix 9. If you need any previous index allowance tables, you should approach the Tax Office responsible for your tax affairs.

In August 2006, Bryony Sullivan sold an investment property she owned for £250,000. The incidental costs of sale amounted to £5,405.

She bought the property in January 1991 for £102,500 including costs of purchase. Central heating was installed in March 1995 for £5,000.

The indexation allowance between January 1991 and April 1998 is 0.249 and from March 1995 to April 1998 it is 0.102.

The chargeable gain, before taper relief, is £111,063 as follows:

	£	£
Sale price		250,000
Less: Costs of sale		5,405
		244,595
Less: Purchase price	102,500	
Enhancement expenditure		
– central heating	5,000	
	107,500	
Indexation allowance:		
£102,500 x 0.249	25,522	
£5,000 x 0.102	510	
		133,532
Chargeable gain, before taper relief		£111,063

Taper relief

The replacement for the indexation allowance is taper relief, the main features of which are:

- The proportion of a chargeable gain that is taxed is determined by reference to the number of whole years (up to a maximum of 10) that an asset was held.

- For this purpose, a year is any continuous period of 12 months.

- Fractions of a year are ignored.

- There are two different percentage tables, one for business assets and one for non-business assets. The reductions for business assets are far more generous than those for non-business assets.

Gains on business assets		Gains on non-business assets	
Number of whole years in qualifying holding period	*Percentage of gain chargeable*	*Number of whole years in qualifying holding period*	*Percentage of gain chargeable*
1	50	1	100
2	25	2	100
3	25	3	95
4	25	4	90
5	25	5	85
6	25	6	80
7	25	7	75
8	25	8	70
9	25	9	65
10 or more	25	**10 or more**	60

For the purposes of these rules the qualifying holding period:

• is the time between the later of the date of acquisition or 6 April 1998 and the date of disposal; or

• is increased by one year for a non-business asset that was acquired before 17 March 1998.

Allowable losses are not tapered. They are set off against chargeable gains before taper relief. The treatment is identical for both losses made in the same tax year as well as those brought forward from earlier years. Effectively, this means that both losses and gains are tapered. Nevertheless, you can choose the way in which you set losses against gains for maximum tax advantage. This means setting them:

• first against any gains on which no taper relief is available; and

• then against any gains where the taper relief is less than on other gains, and so on.

The indexation allowance is a deduction in arriving at the amount of a gain. This contrasts with taper relief, which is given after the chargeable gain has been calculated. Therefore, in circumstances where a chargeable gain arises on a disposal to which both indexation allowance and taper relief apply:

• the indexation allowance is first of all taken off to arrive at the amount of gain;

• then any allowable losses are deducted; and

• finally, taper relief is given on the net amount of the gain.

Business assets

As illustrated in the table in the previous section, the rate of taper relief applied to gains on disposals of business assets is far more generous than the reduction for non-business assets.

The assets which qualify for the enhanced rate of taper relief applicable to business assets are:

- *assets used by a partnership of which you are a member and in other limited circumstances;

- †assets used in your trade or by a company in which you have a qualifying shareholding;

- †any of your assets used in your job where you work for a trading employer;

- †all shareholdings held by employees and others in unquoted trading companies;

- †all shareholdings held by employees in quoted trading companies;

- †shareholdings in a quoted trading company where the holder is not an employee but can exercise at least 5% of the voting rights;

- shares owned by employees and office holders of a non-trading company provided the employee does not have a material interest in the company. This is defined as a right to more than 10% of:

    — the profit;

    — the assets on winding up;

    — the voting rights;

    — any class of share capital.

* The qualifying criteria were introduced from 6 April 2004.

† The qualifying criteria under these headings were relaxed from 6 April 2000.

Where an asset only satisfies the definition of a business asset from either 6 April 2000 or 6 April 2004, it will be regarded as a non-business asset up to that date. Accordingly, the gain on disposal must be time apportioned:

- over the period of ownership; or

- from 6 April 1998, if later, so that part of the gain is treated as a gain qualifying for business asset taper relief with the balance as a non-business asset.

Martin Osborne bought a shareholding in his employer's quoted company in August 1998 for £4,970. His stake in the company is not significant. He sold the shares in February 2007 for £20,000.

The shares only qualified as a business asset for taper relief purposes from 6 April 2000. Therefore, the gain must be apportioned throughout the period of ownership.

Martin's total net chargeable gain for 2006/07 is £5,084 as follows:

	£	£
Sale proceeds of shares		20,000
Less: Cost price		4,970
Gain before taper relief		£15,030

(a) Period as non-business asset

$$\frac{\text{August 1998 to April 2000}}{\text{August 1998 to February 2007}} = \frac{20 \text{ months}}{102 \text{ months}} \times £15,030 = \quad 2,947$$

Less: Taper relief – 30% (eight years)	884
Chargeable gain	£2,063

(b) Period as business asset

$$\frac{\text{April 2000 to February 2007}}{\text{August 1998 to February 2007}} = \frac{82 \text{ months}}{102 \text{ months}} \times £15,030 = \quad 12,083$$

Less: Taper relief – 75% (seven years)	9,062
Chargeable gain	£3,021

Assets owned on 31 March 1982

Gains and losses on disposals of assets that you held on 31 March 1982 can be calculated solely by reference to their market value at that date, ignoring original costs. In most cases, these rules mean your capital gains will be reduced compared to a calculation based on historical cost only.

Ashley Barker acquired a freehold factory in the late 1970s for £25,000. It was valued at £30,000 on 31 March 1982. Ashley sold the factory in May 2006 for £120,000.

The indexation allowance between March 1982 and April 1998 is 1.047.

The chargeable gain is £38,084 as follows:

	On 31 March 1982 Value		On Historical Cost	
	£	£	£	£
Sale price		120,000		120,000
Less: March 1982 value	30,000		—	
Acquisition cost	—		25,000	
Indexation allowance				
£30,000 x 1.047	31,410		31,410	
		61,410		56,410
		£58,590		£63,590
Lesser gain			58,590	
Less: Taper relief – 35%			20,506	
2006/07 chargeable gain			£38,084	

As might be expected there are special rules where the computations based first on the March 1982 value, and second on historical cost, give different results, as follows:

On March 1982 Value	On Historical Cost	Chargeable Gain/Loss
Gain of £6,170	Gain of £4,280	£4,280 Gain
Loss of £8,410	Loss of £7,035	£7,035 Loss
Loss of £1,690	Gain of £3,380	neither gain nor loss
Gain of £5,720	Loss of £960	neither gain nor loss

You can, however, elect for the capital gains on all disposals of assets you owned on 31 March 1982 to be calculated just by reference to their values at that date and ignoring original costs. Once made, this election cannot be revoked.

Assets held on 6 April 1965

You will only need to know how to calculate the capital gain on the disposal of an asset you owned on 6 April 1965:

- if you have not made an election for the 31 March 1982 value to be used; or

- in the highly unlikely situation that the value at 6 April 1965 is greater than the 31 March 1982 market price.

In such circumstances I recommend you take professional advice.

Investments in shares

Before 6 April 1982 each shareholding was considered as a single asset and known as a 'pool' of shares. Every purchase of the same class of shares, or a sale of the part of the holding, represented either an addition to, or a disposal out of, the 'pool'. This changed when the indexation allowance was introduced. From 6 April 1982 each shareholding acquired was considered to be a separate asset. A further purchase of shares of a holding owned by you at 5 April 1982 could not be added to the 'pool'.

The rules were amended from 6 April 1985. Shares of the same class were again treated as a single asset growing or diminishing on each acquisition or disposal. This form of 'pooling' applied to shares acquired after 5 April 1982 unless they had already been disposed of before 6 April 1985. It is called a 'new holding'.

A 'pool' which was frozen under the 1982 rules has to stay that way. It continues as a single asset which cannot grow by subsequent acquisitions and is known as a '1982 holding'.

A '1982 holding' is treated like any other asset in working out entitlement to the indexation allowance. This is not so for a 'new holding'. It had to be continuingly indexed each time there was an addition to, or a disposal out of, the 'pool' up until April 1998.

All forms of 'pooling' ceased for shares acquired on or after 6 April 1998. This is when taper relief was introduced and from which date it is necessary to record and retain the date of acquisition of each holding of shares.

The procedure for matching shares sold with their corresponding acquisition is as follows:

- shares acquired on the same day;

- shares acquired within 30 days following a disposal;

- shares acquired before the disposal, but after 5 April 1998, identifying the most recent acquisitions first;

- shares comprised in a 'new holding', the 1982–98 share pool;

- shares within a '1982 holding', the 1965–82 share pool;

- any shares acquired before 6 April 1965, last in first out; or

- shares acquired more than 30 days after the disposal.

Josephine Power bought 3,000 shares in a quoted company on 18 February 1999 at a total cost of £6,700. She sold the entire holding on 19 January 2007 for £11,720. She reacquired the same number of shares in the company on 7 February 2007 for £11,110.

As the repurchase took place within 30 days of the sale the chargeable gain is £620 as follows:

	£
Sale of 3,000 shares on 19 January 2007	11,720
Less: Cost of reacquisition on 7 February 2007	11,100
Chargeable gain	£620

Laurence Stone made the following purchases in the shares of a quoted company:

Date	Number of Shares	Cost
June 1978	3,000	£4,500
November 1987	3,500	£7,875
September 1994	1,500	£4,875
August 2002	4,000	£14,000

In July 2006 he sold 10,000 shares for £40,000. The shares were valued at £1.75 on 31 March 1982. The indexation allowance is:

1.047 between March 1982 and April 1998

0.402 between November 1987 and September 1994

0.121 between September 1994 and April 1998

4,000 shares sold must first of all be identified with the acquisition after 5 April 1998 as follows:

	£
Cost of 4,000 shares in August 2002	14,000
Proceeds of sale of 4,000 shares	16,000
	2,000
Less: Taper relief – 5%	100
Chargeable gain	£1,900

Second, 5,000 shares sold must be identified with those in the 'new holding' as follows:

	£
Cost of 3,500 shares in November 1987	7,875
Indexation allowance to September 1994 – 0.402	3,165
	11,040
Cost of 1,500 shares in September 1994	4,875
	15,915
Indexation allowance to April 1998 – 0.121	1,925
	17,840

Proceeds of sale of 5,000 shares	20,000
	2,160
Less: Taper relief – 35%	756
Chargeable gain	£1,404

The remaining 1,000 shares sold are then identified with part of the shares acquired before 31 March 1982. As the cost was £1.50 per share it is beneficial to calculate the capital gain on the share price at 31 March 1982 as follows:

	£
Value of 1,000 shares at March 1982	1,750
Indexation allowance to April 1998 – 1.047	1,832
	3,582
Proceeds of sale of 1,000 shares	4,000
	418
Less: Taper relief – 35%	146
Chargeable gain	£272

The total chargeable gain on the sale is £3,576.

Whenever you receive a free or bonus issue of shares of the same class as an existing holding the date of their acquisition is the same as that of the original holding. The same principle applies to further shares acquired under a rights issue.

Where a company in which you have a holding is taken over and you receive:

- shares in the new company in exchange for your shares in the company taken over, no disposal for tax purposes takes place at that time. Your new holding is regarded as having being acquired at the same time, and for the same price, as the old one; or

- a mixture of cash and shares in the new company, a gain or a loss arises on the cash element of the takeover. It is then necessary to apportion the cost price of the old shares, including any indexation allowance up to the date of the takeover, between the cash received and the value of the shareholding in the new company at the time.

Your home

The profit on the sale of your home is free of tax. The exemption automatically covers the house and the garden or grounds up to half a hectare, including the land on which the house is built. A larger area can qualify for exemption where it can be shown that it was required for the enjoyment of the house.

Where a home has not been lived in as your private residence throughout the full period of ownership or, if later, since 31 March 1982, a proportion of the gain on sale is taxable. Certain periods of absence are, however, disregarded in determining whether the gain is totally tax free. These are:

- the last three years of ownership always; and

- generally when you have to live away from home because of your work.

Guy Robinson sold his home in February 2007, making a profit of £90,000 as worked out for Capital Gains Tax purposes. He had bought the property in November 1990.

His job had taken him abroad between March 2001 and May 2003. Shortly after his return he bought a new home and moved there in August 2003.

The time spent working abroad and the last 36 months from February 2004 are considered periods when the property was Guy's main residence. The chargeable gain is, therefore, restricted to the part of the gain apportioned to the six months between August 2003 and February 2004 as follows:

$$\frac{\text{Chargeable period}}{\text{Period of ownership}} = \frac{6 \text{ months}}{75 \text{ months}} \times £90,000 = £7,200$$

Where part of your home is used exclusively for business purposes, such as a surgery or office, the proportion of the profit on sale attributable to the business use:

• is a chargeable gain; and

• qualifies for the enhanced rate of taper relief for business assets.

If, during your period of ownership, a property is partly lived in as your home and rented out for the remainder of the time, the gain attributable to the period of letting which is exempt is the lower of:

• either £40,000; or

• an amount equivalent to the gain on the part you have occupied as your home.

Harriet Underwood made a taxable profit of £85,000 when she sold her flat in May 2006. She had acquired the property in April 1999 but only lived there from April 2003 until it was sold. For the remainder of the time the property was rented out. The chargeable gain is only £8,250 as follows:

	£	£
Capital gain (period of ownership – 85 months)		85,000
Less: Main residence exemption – 37 months	37,000	
Letting exemption – 48 months (lower of £40,000 or £37,000)	37,000	
		74,000
		11,000
Less: Taper relief – 25%		2,750
Chargeable gain		£8,250

A second home

It is not uncommon these days for individuals to have two properties. The main home is usually a house or flat within a commutable distance from the office or other place of work. The second property might be in the country, by the seaside or abroad in a warmer climate.

It is only the profit on the sale of your main residence which is tax free. Which one of your two or more homes is considered your main residence is usually a matter of fact. It is, however, possible for you to determine this in writing to your Tax Office. In the election you should state which of your homes you want regarded as your principal private residence for Capital Gains Tax purposes. The election can:

- commence from the date when you first have at least two homes available to you; or

- apply from any time in the two years starting with the commencement date;

- be made retrospectively on any date within two years of the commencement date; or

- be varied as and when it suits you.

Husband and wife living together are only allowed one qualifying home between them. The same applies to civil partners.

Pradeep and Sonia Singh bought their first home in January 2001 for £120,000. Not long afterwards Sonia received an inheritance from her father's estate and, with some of the money, they decided to buy a small flat by the seaside. This cost them £70,000 in October 2002. They elected for their first home to be their principal private residence for Capital Gains Tax purposes. In March 2007 they sold their holiday flat for £150,000, realizing a profit of £80,000. In order to reduce their tax bill they changed their main residence election to the holiday flat for the final four weeks up to the date of sale. The taxable gain, split equally between them, is £23,094 as follows:

	£
Profit on sale	80,000
Less: Main residence relief (last 3 years)	
$\dfrac{36 \text{ months}}{53 \text{ months}} \times £80,000$	54,340
	25,660
Less: Taper relief – 10%	2,566
Chargeable gain	£23,094

If you own a home which was occupied rent-free by the same dependant relative both on 5 April 1988 and throughout your period of ownership, then the profit on the sale is tax free.

Chattels

Profits from selling chattels with an expected life of more than 50 years and which are sold for less than £6,000 are tax free. Chattels include paintings and other works of art, antiques, furniture, jewellery, stamps and ornaments. Articles comprising a set are considered as a single item when they are sold to the same person but at different times.

For items which fetch between £6,000 and £15,000, the chargeable gain is restricted to 5/3 times the amount by which the proceeds of sale (ignoring expenses) exceeds £6,000 where this is to your advantage.

Meryl Nichols sold an antique vase at auction in March 2007 for £10,500, receiving £9,750 after expenses of sale.

She had inherited the vase from her mother when she died in April 1987. It was then valued at only £1,000.

The indexation allowance between April 1987 and April 1998 is 0.597.

The chargeable gain is £4,875 as follows:

	£	£
Net sale price		9,750
Less: Acquisition cost	1,000	
Indexation allowance at 0.597	597	1,597
Gain		£8,153
But restricted to $5/3$ x £4,500 (£10,500 – £6,000)		7,500
Less: Taper relief – 35%		2,625
Chargeable gain		£4,875

When an article is sold for under £6,000 and at a loss, the allowable loss is restricted by assuming the sale proceeds were equal to £6,000.

Vincent Wells bought a set of stamps in the late 1980s for £8,300. The set was sold in December 2006 for £6,600. Vincent's allowable loss is £1,700. If he had only made £3,800 on the sale, the tax loss would have been £2,300 (£8,300 – £6,000).

Gifts and valuations

There are times when a figure different from the actual disposal proceeds is used in the calculation of a capital gain. This happens, for example, when you make a gift or sell an asset at a nominal value to a close member of your family. On these occasions you must work out the capital gain based on the open-market value of the asset at the time of gift or disposal.

Whenever you need to use valuations to work out the gain or loss in such circumstances, there is a free service from HMRC which will help you complete your Self-Assessment Tax Return.

You may ask your Tax Office to check valuations after you have made the disposal but before you make your return:

- you can ask for one copy of form CG34 for each valuation you want confirmed; and

- you must then return the completed form to your Tax Office together with all the other information and documents requested on the form.

Agreed valuations will not subsequently be challenged when you submit your Tax Return unless you did not previously mention important facts affecting the valuations. If your figures are not agreed, HMRC will put forward alternative valuations.

Where the gift is one of a business asset, you can elect jointly with the transferee for payment of the tax on the gift to be postponed until the asset is subsequently disposed of by the transferee.

Short life assets

Short life, or wasting, assets are those with an expected lifespan of less than 50 years. A gain on the disposal of a wasting asset is worked out in the same way as that on the disposal of any other asset, except that the purchase price wastes away during the expected lifespan of the asset.

Leases of land for less than 50 years are wasting assets. There is a specific formula for calculating the proportion of the purchase price of a lease that can be deducted from the sale proceeds.

The gain or loss on the sale of a wasting asset that is also 'tangible moveable property' is outside of tax.

Part disposals

Where you dispose of only part of an asset that you own:

- You apportion the acquisition cost between the part sold and the fraction retained. This is worked out on a pro-rata basis by reference to the sale proceeds of the part sold and the open-market value of the proportion retained.

- Any indexation allowance due is worked out on the cost of the part sold.

- The proportion of cost price of the asset attributable to the part retained can be set against the proceeds on the sale of the remainder at a later date.

- If the part sold is small compared with the value of the whole asset you can simply deduct the sale proceeds from the acquisition cost. Where the part disposal is one of land this procedure can be followed so long as the sale proceeds are both less than £20,000 and one-fifth of the value of the remaining land.

Enterprise Investment Scheme

A profit on disposing of qualifying shares under the Enterprise Investment Scheme (EIS) is free of Capital Gains Tax, provided:

- the Income Tax relief originally allowed on the investment has not been withdrawn; and

- the disposal takes place at least three years after the issue of the shares.

If you incur a loss on disposing of qualifying shares you can offset the loss against either:

- capital gains in the same year that the loss is realized; or

- your taxable income in the year of loss, or the previous year.

It is also possible to defer Capital Gains Tax payable on chargeable gains by reinvesting the gains in qualifying EIS shares. For deferral relief purposes the chargeable gains must be reinvested in the period beginning one year before, and ending three years after, the original disposal. Deferral relief can be claimed:

- along with both Income Tax relief (see Chapter 10) and exemption from Capital Gains Tax (as above) up to an annual investment limit of £400,000; or

- on its own as the amount of gains that can be deferred is unlimited; or

- in any other combination you choose within the rules.

If deferral relief is claimed the original liability to Capital Gains Tax will crystallize when the EIS shares are sold.

Venture Capital Trusts

A disposal of shares in a Venture Capital Trust (VCT) is exempt from Capital Gains Tax provided:

- the original cost of the shares disposed of did not exceed the maximum permitted investment limit in the year of purchase, £200,000 for 2006/07; and

- the company qualifies as a VCT both at the time the shares are acquired and at the date of disposal.

Inheritances

No Capital Gains Tax is payable on the unrealized profits on your assets as at the date of your death. When you inherit an asset you acquire it at the value on the date of death of the deceased. Generally, this rule is also applied whenever you become entitled to assets from a Trust.

14 COMPLETING THE RETURN AND CALCULATING YOUR TAX

When you collect your post from the doormat you can always pick out your Tax Return from the other letters. It comes at the same time every year in a thin cellophane envelope with the instruction 'Please open immediately'. This book is being published around the date when you can expect to receive your Tax Return asking for information about your income and capital gains for the year ended 5 April 2007, as well as the allowances and reliefs you want to claim in the same year. The standard ten-page return comes with:

- guidance notes;
- supplementary pages based on your tax history; and
- a tax calculation guide.

The additional colour-coded supplementary pages specific to the income and gains of the taxpayer are:

1.	Employment	Pink
2.	Share schemes	Purple
3.	Self-employment	Orange
4.	Partnership	Turquoise
5.	Land and property	Red
6.	Foreign income, gains and tax credit relief	Mustard
7.	Trusts, settlements and the estates of deceased persons	Brown
8.	Capital gains	Light blue
9.	Non-residence	Green
10.	Pensions – taxable lump sums	Dark blue

There are no supplementary pages for UK investment income which is entered on the main Return.

There is now a short four-page Tax Return for taxpayers with uncompli-cated affairs such as:

- employees, but not company directors, with taxable benefits-in-kind;

- the self-employed with a business where the annual turnover is less than £15,000;

- pensioners in receipt of State Retirement Pension, a pension from a former employer or an annuity; and

- taxpayers receiving straightforward investment income or a small amount of income from property.

You will only be sent this shortened version on the basis of the infor-mation on your 2005/06 Tax Return and providing your affairs fit into a tightly drawn set of criteria.

When you receive your Return try to avoid the temptation to put it to one side. There is no advantage in delaying. It is better to get started sooner because you will:

- have more time to get help from HMRC if you need it;

- have more time to save money for any tax you have to pay;

- find out earlier if you are due a tax refund; and

- get a big weight off your mind!!

Start by filling in page 2. This tells you which supplementary pages you will need. These can either be obtained by telephoning the Orderline on 0845 9000 404 (open 7 days a week from 8 a.m. to 10 p.m) or from the HMRC website. Alternatively you can send a fax to 0845 9000 604. The supplementary pages come with Notes to help you fill in the pages you requested. Help Sheets and leaflets giving more detailed information about particular tax rules for working out the income or capital gains to be declared on the supplementary pages are referred to in the Notes and are also available from the Orderline.

Then you should decide if you want to calculate your tax or if you want your tax office to do it for you. Remember the deadlines:

30 September 2007

You must send back your completed Tax Return for the year to 5 April 2007 to your tax office by then if you want HMRC to:

- calculate your tax in time for you to make payment on 31 January 2008; or

- collect tax owing of less than £2,000 through your tax code. This deadline is extended to 31 December 2007 if your Tax Return is filed over the internet.

31 January 2008

This date is important for three reasons. By then you must:

- let your tax office have your completed Return;

- pay the balance of any tax you owe for the 2006/07 tax year (unless it is to be collected through your tax code); and

- if appropriate pay your first payment on account for the 2007/08 tax year.

You are now ready to complete the remainder of your Tax Return. Begin by gathering together all the information for the year ended 5 April 2007 on your income, capital gains, reliefs and allowances from the records you have been keeping for the year.

Keeping proper records

For most kinds of income and capital gains you will only need to keep the records given to you by whoever provided that income. This means for those of you

- in employment:

  — your Form P60, a certificate your employer will give you after 5 April (the end of the tax year) showing details of pay and tax deducted;

  — any Form P45 (part 1A), a certificate from an employer showing details of pay and tax from a job you have left;

  — any Form P160 (part 1A) you may have been given when you retire and go on to receive a pension paid by your former employer;

  — your payslips or pay statements;

  — a note of the amount of any tips or gratuities and details of any other taxable receipts. You are advised to record these as soon as possible after you receive them, not simply estimate them at the end of the year;

— Form P11D or P9D or equivalent information from all the employers you have worked for during the year, showing any benefits-in-kind and expenses payments given to you.

- receiving a UK pension or social security benefits:

  — your Form P60, a certificate which may be given to you by the payer of your occupational pension, showing the amount of your pension and the tax deducted;

  — any other certificate of a pension you received and the tax deducted from it;

  — details given to you by the Department of Work and Pensions (DWP) relating to state pensions, taxable state benefits, statutory sick pay, statutory maternity or paternity pay and the jobseeker's allowance.

- in business or letting property:

  — please refer to Chapter 7 and the section on Records.

- receiving investment income:

  — bank and building society statements or passbooks;

  — statements of interest and any other income received from your savings and investments; for example, an annuity;

  — any tax deduction certificates supplied by your bank or building society;

  — dividend vouchers received from UK companies;

  — unit trust tax vouchers;

  — life insurance chargeable events certificates;

  — details of any income you received from a trust.

It is also sensible to keep details of any exceptional amounts – such as an inheritance or other windfall – which you receive and invest.

- making capital gains or losses:

  — contracts for the purchase or sale of shares, unit trusts, property or other assets;

  — copies of any valuations taken into account in your calculation of capital gains or losses;

— bills, invoices or other evidence of payment records such as bank statements and cheque stubs for costs you claim for the purchase, improvement or sale of assets;

— details of any assets you have given away or put into a trust.

• claiming personal allowances, other deductions or reliefs:

— certificates of interest paid;

— court orders or other legally binding maintenance agreements;

— declarations you have made to charities of gifts under Gift Aid;

— receipts for the payment of pension premiums;

— a birth certificate for any claim where age is relevant;

— a marriage certificate where the married couple's allowance is being claimed;

— notification that you registered as a blind person.

These are some examples of the types of records you would be advised to keep. The list is not exhaustive and does not cover every situation. If you are in any doubt, ask your tax office or Tax Enquiry Centre for advice.

The period for which you must keep your records is:

• five years from the latest date by which your Tax Return has to be filed if you are self-employed, in partnership or are letting property;

• in any other case the first 31 January anniversary following the tax year.

Even if you do not have all the information you need do not let this deter you from preparing your Tax Return and sending it back to your tax office. Of course, you must do all you can to get the information, but if you are unable to provide final figures when the time comes to send off your Tax Return then estimate the missing amounts. Tick box 23.2 on page 9 of your Return and describe in the space provided at 23.9:

• which figures are provisional. You should refer to the appropriate box numbers on your Tax Return or any of the other supplementary pages you have completed;

• why you could not give final figures; and

• when you expect to be able to provide your tax office with the correct information.

Your tax office will not normally regard a Tax Return as incomplete just because it contains provisional details of income or capital gains provided you have taken all reasonable measures to obtain the final figures, and you make sure that you send them as soon as they are available.

Completing the Return

You must answer all the questions. If you answer 'Yes' you should fill in the boxes that apply to you, otherwise move on to the next question.

Always

- write only in the space provided using blue or black ink;
- only use numbers when you are asked for amounts; and
- do not include pence.

There is just not enough space for me to reproduce all the supplementary pages and the core ten-page Tax Return in the Guide. I have therefore decided to reproduce the front of the supplementary page on Employment and most of pages 3 to 10 of the Tax Return.

If you have more than one job you will need to fill in a separate copy of the Employment page for each employment. In box 1.8 enter your before-tax salary or wage from your form P60. Enter the tax deducted by your employer in box 1.11. The amounts of any benefits-in-kind, which are taxable, will have been worked out by your employer and can be clearly identified from the copy of your form P11D which will be given to you. Enter these benefits and expenses, if appropriate, in boxes 1.12 to 1.23. The reverse of the employment page deals with:

- lump sums and compensation payments;
- foreign earnings;
- expenses you incurred in doing your job; and
- repayments of student loans.

If you received income from UK savings and investments tick the 'Yes' box at the top of page 3 of your Tax Return. You then need to complete boxes 10.1 to 10.26 as appropriate. The page is divided into two halves:

- Interest:

  Take note that there are two boxes 10.1 and 10.8 which specifically deal with interest you have received from UK banks, building societies or National Savings where no tax has been deducted.

Income for the year, ended 5 April 2007

HM Revenue & Customs

EMPLOYMENT

Fill in these boxes first

Name
Simon Black

Tax reference
43296 55434

If you want help, look up the box numbers in the Notes.

Details of employer

Employer's PAYE reference - the 'HM Revenue & Customs office number and reference' on your P60 or 'PAYE reference' on your P45

1.1 28/B 604

Employer's name
1.2 Broadwood Engineers Ltd

Date employment started
(only if between 6 April 2006 and 5 April 2007)
1.3 / /

Date employment finished
(only if between 6 April 2006 and 5 April 2007)
1.4 / /

Employer's address
1.5 Bridge Street
Broadwood

Tick box 1.6 if you were a director of the company
1.6

and, if so, tick box 1.7 if it was a close company
1.7

Postcode PT3 7GN

Income from employment

■ **Money** - see Notes, page EN3.

Before tax

● Payments from P60 (or P45)   **1.8** £ 22,152-00

● Payments not on P60, etc.   - tips   **1.9** £

  - other payments (excluding expenses entered below and lump sums and compensation payments or benefits entered overleaf)   **1.10** £

Tax taken off

● UK tax taken off payments in boxes 1.8 to 1.10   **1.11** £ 4,580-84

■ **Benefits and expenses** - see Notes, pages EN3 to EN6. If any benefits connected with termination of employment were received, or enjoyed, after that termination and were from a **former** employer you need Help Sheet IR204, available from the Orderline. Do not enter such benefits here.

● Assets transferred/ payments made for you   Amount   **1.12** £

● Vans   Amount   **1.18** £

● Vouchers, credit cards and tokens   Amount   **1.13** £

● Interest-free and low-interest loans see Notes, page EN5.   Amount   **1.19** £

● Living accommodation   Amount   **1.14** £

box 1.20 is not used.

● Excess mileage allowance and passenger payments   Amount   **1.15** £

● Private medical or dental insurance   Amount   **1.21** £ 500

● Company cars   **1.16** £ 1,800

● Other benefits   Amount   **1.22** £

● Fuel for company cars   Amount   **1.17** £ 2,160

● Expenses payments received and balancing charges   Amount   **1.23** £

SAT01

INCOME *for the year ended 5 April 2007*

Q10 **Did you receive any income from UK savings and investments?** **YES** ✓

If yes, tick this box and then fill in boxes 10.1 to 10.26 as appropriate. Include only your share of any joint savings and investments. If not applicable, go to Question 11.

■ *Interest and alternative finance receipts*

● Interest and alternative finance receipts from UK banks or building societies including UK internet accounts.
If you have more than one bank or building society account enter totals in the boxes.

- enter any bank or building society interest and alternative finance receipts that **have not had tax taken off**. (Interest and alternative finance receipts are usually taxed before you receive them so make sure you should be filling in box 10.1, rather than boxes 10.2 to 10.4.) Enter other types of interest and alternative finance receipts in boxes 10.5 to 10.14, as appropriate.

Taxable amount
10.1 £

- enter details of **taxed** bank or building society interest and **taxed** alternative finance receipts. *The Working Sheet on page 11 of your Tax Return Guide will help you fill in boxes 10.2 to 10.4.*

	Amount **after** tax taken off	Tax taken off	Gross amount **before** tax
	10.2 £ *288*	**10.3** £ *72*	**10.4** £ *360*

● Interest distributions from UK authorised unit trusts and open-ended investment companies (dividend distributions go below)

	Amount **after** tax taken off	Tax taken off	Gross amount **before** tax
	10.5 £	**10.6** £	**10.7** £

● National Savings & Investments (other than First Option Bonds and Fixed Rate Savings Bonds and the first £70 of interest from an Ordinary Account)

Taxable amount
10.8 £ *400*

● National Savings & Investments First Option Bonds and Fixed Rate Savings Bonds

	Amount **after** tax taken off	Tax taken off	Gross amount **before** tax
	10.9 £ *160*	**10.10** £ *40*	**10.11** £ *200*

● Other income from UK savings and investments (except dividends)

	Amount **after** tax taken off	Tax taken off	Gross amount **before** tax
	10.12 £	**10.13** £	**10.14** £

■ *Dividends*

● Dividends and other qualifying distributions from UK companies (enter distributions from the tax exempt profits of a Real Estate Investment Trust at Q13)

	Dividend/distribution	Tax credit	Dividend/distribution **plus** credit
	10.15 £ *450*	**10.16** £ *50*	**10.17** £ *500*

● Dividend distributions from UK authorised unit trusts and open-ended investment companies

	Dividend/distribution	Tax credit	Dividend/distribution **plus** credit
	10.18 £ *288*	**10.19** £ *32*	**10.20** £ *320*

● Stock dividends from UK companies

	Dividend	Notional tax	Dividend **plus** notional tax
	10.21 £ *54*	**10.22** £ *6*	**10.23** £ *60*

● Non-qualifying distributions and loans written off

	Distribution/loan	Notional tax	Taxable amount
	10.24 £	**10.25** £	**10.26** £

- Dividends:

  Dividends on your shareholdings come with counterfoils. These show the amount of the dividend and the accompanying tax credit. It is the total of all of your dividends in the year, and tax credits, which should be entered in boxes 10.15 and 10.16. Add these totals together to get the 'dividend/distribution plus credit' figure to be shown in box 10.17. The same procedure should be followed for all other dividends that you have received including those on your unit trust investments and 'scrip' dividends from UK companies. A 'scrip' dividend is where you take up an offer of shares instead of a cash dividend.

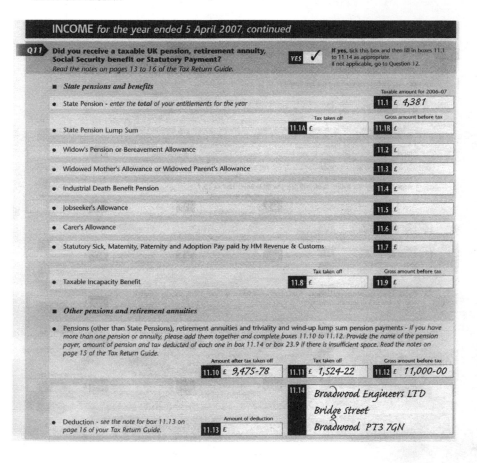

Did you receive a taxable UK pension, retirement annuity or Social Security benefit in 2006/07? If your pension or benefit is taxable and should be included on the Return tick the 'Yes' box at the top of page 4 and fill in boxes 11.1 to 11.14, as appropriate. As with the Employment page the amount of your pension from a previous employer's pension fund, and the tax deducted throughout the year, will also be shown on a form P60 which has been sent to you. If you are drawing the state pension you should declare the amount of your pension for the 52-week period to 5 April 2007. Particularly where the pension is paid quarterly, there will be a small difference between the income you should declare on the Return and the actual pension received during the tax year. Do not include either the £10 Christmas Bonus or your winter fuel payment as these are not taxable.

Question 12 will only be of any concern to you if you received any of the following kinds of income:

- gains on UK life insurance policies, life annuities or capital redemption policies; or

- refunds of surplus additional voluntary contributions.

If you do not need to tick the 'Yes' box you can go straight to question 13 which asks you whether you received any other income that has not already been entered elsewhere on your Tax Return. This would include, for example:

- any casual earnings not declared elsewhere;

- accrued income on a transfer of securities;

- income received after your business has ceased; or

- benefits received when you have owned, or contributed to the acquisition of, property (pre-owned assets).

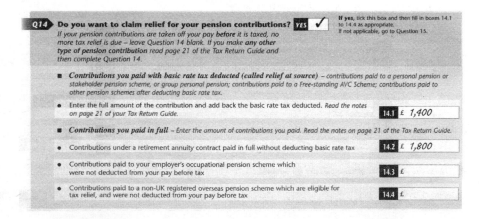

Question 14 is the first in the section dealing with reliefs for the year ended 5 April 2007 and is relevant if you want to claim relief for pension contributions.

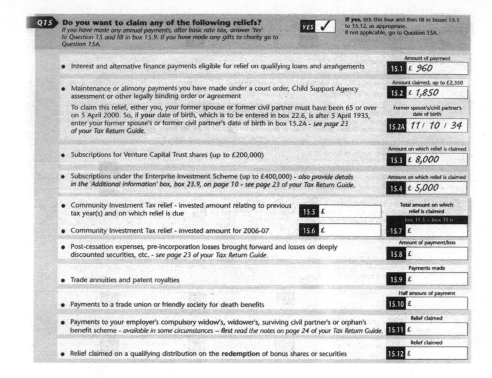

Question 15 lists a number of reliefs. Do you want to claim any of them? They include:

- interest paid on qualifying loans;

- maintenance or alimony payments you are making;

- your subscriptions for new ordinary shares in a Venture Capital Trust;

- subscriptions under the Enterprise Investment Scheme;

- expenses incurred on your business, but after it has ceased trading; and

- payments to a trade union or friendly society for death benefits;

- some other miscellaneous reliefs.

You may be entitled to higher-rate tax relief on donations to charities under Gift Aid. Such payments are regarded as having been made by you after tax at the basic rate has been deducted. No further tax relief is due unless you pay tax the the top rate of 40%.

You should enter in boxes 15A.1 and 15A.2 (as appropriate) the amount of any payments made by you in the year to 5 April 2007, even if you are not claiming higher-rate tax relief.

Perhaps by the time you complete your Tax Return and send it back to your Tax Office you have made Gift Aid donations in the 2007/08 tax year starting on 6 April 2007. You can elect to have those payments treated as though they were made in the year to 5 April 2007. You can do so by entering the amount of such payments in box 15A.4. Similarly, any payments made in 2006/07 and related back to 2005/06 should be entered in box 15A.3 of the form.

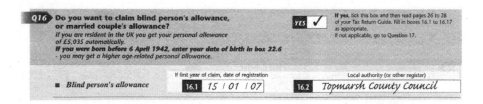

Q15A Have you made any gifts to charity?	YES ✓	If yes, tick this box and then read page 25 of your Tax Return Guide. Fill in boxes 15A.1 to 15A.7 as appropriate. If not applicable, go to Question 16.
• Gift Aid payments, including covenanted payments to charities, made between 6 April 2006 and 5 April 2007	15A.1 £	1,800
• The total of any 'one-off' payments included in box 15A.1	15A.2 £	1,200
• Gift Aid payments made after 5 April 2006 but treated as if made in the tax year 2005–06	15A.3 £	600
• Gift Aid payments made after 5 April 2007 but to be treated as if made in the tax year 2006–07	15A.4 £	800
• Total relief claimed in 2006–07	15A.5 £	box 15.A1 + box 15A.4 minus box 15A.3
• Gifts of qualifying investments to charities – shares and securities	15A.6 £	3,000
• Gifts of qualifying investments to charities – real property	15A.7 £	

Question 16 is devoted to the allowances for the year ended 5 April 2007 which you may want to claim. There are separate sections covering all the personal allowances and the individuals – whether they be single, married, in a civil partnership or elderly – who can claim them. In each case there is a space for you to enter the information HMRC need to make sure you are given the full and right tax allowances.

Q16 Do you want to claim blind person's allowance, or married couple's allowance?		YES ✓	If yes, tick this box and then read pages 26 to 28 of your Tax Return Guide. Fill in boxes 16.1 to 16.17 as appropriate.
If you are resident in the UK you get your personal allowance of £5,035 automatically. If you were born before 6 April 1942, enter your date of birth in box 22.6 - you may get a higher age-related personal allowance.			If not applicable, go to Question 17.

	If first year of claim, date of registration		Local authority (or other register)
■ Blind person's allowance	16.1	15 / 01 / 07	16.2 Topmarsh County Council

The first part of this section is for you to make a claim for the special blind person's allowance. You will need to give the name of the local authority, or equivalent body, with whom you have registered your blindness as well as the date of registration.

Then comes the section on claiming the married couple's allowance. This can only be claimed if either you, your husband, wife or civil partner, were born before 6 April 1935. So you can only claim the allowance in 2006/07 if either of you had reached 65 years of age before 6 April 2000.

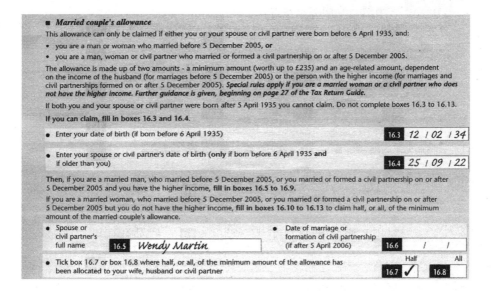

The section at the top of page 7 is about transferring surplus allowances.

The remainder of the Return asks for other information for the year ended 5 April 2007 and is all relatively straightforward. When the Return is finished it must be signed and dated in the space provided on page 10. Bear in mind the wording of the declaration: 'The information I have given in this Tax Return is correct and complete to the best of my knowledge and belief'. Then send the form back to your tax office. As there is no space in each section of the Return you may well need to prepare separate statements of, for example, your interest and dividend income in order to arrive at the single figures which need to be entered on the Return. I strongly recommend that copies of any supporting statements or schedules which you prepare should be sent to your tax office along with the Return. Do not, however, send in any building society statements, dividend vouchers and other financial records. Just keep them safely.

If, after you have sent off your Tax Return, you find that you have made a mistake, let your tax office know at once so that it can be taken into account.

Calculating your tax

You should receive a Tax Calculation Guide with your Tax Return. This will help you if you want to calculate your tax. If your tax affairs are more complicated you will need to ask for the Comprehensive Tax Calculation Guide. The key steps in calculating your tax bill are as follows:

- bring together all the non-savings income you have entered on your Return;

- total the deductions and allowances you have claimed for the year;

- add your savings and dividend income to arrive at your total income, take away your deductions and allowances to get your taxable income, then work out the tax due, so far;

- take off further allowances, deductions and tax paid at source – then work out your total Income Tax, Class 4 National Insurance Contributions (if you are self-employed or in partnership) and any Student Loan Repayments – to give you the figure to enter in box 18.3 on page 7 of your Return;

- work out what you have to pay for 2006/07 by 31 January 2008;

- calculate any 2007/08 payments on account you may have to make on 31 January and 31 July 2008.

George Salmon is employed by a local company as a senior engineer. Since the beginning of July 1997 he has regularly been asked to speak at seminars and write articles for trade magazines. George is 54 (he was born on 8 February 1953) and is happily married to Lynne. They do not have any children. He owns a modest number of investments and his spare cash is deposited in National Savings and building society accounts.

George files his Tax Return for the year to 5 April 2007 on 23 October 2007. It shows the following entries:

	£	Box Number in Return
(1) Employment		
Salary	39,000.00	1.8
Tax deducted by employer	9,926.00	1.11
Subscription to the Association		
of Mechanical Engineers	100.00	1.34
Company car benefit	3,700.00	1.16
Fuel benefit for company car	2,880.00	1.17
(2) Self-Employment		
Adjusted profit shown by the accounts		
for the year to 30 June 2006	10,000.00	3.92
(3) Pension premiums paid in 2006/07		
(based on self-employed earnings –		
gross equivalent)	2,500.00	14.9
(4) Savings Income		
National Savings Income Bonds (paid gross)	250.00	10.8
Building Society interest received		
– gross interest	600.00	10.4
– tax deducted	120.00	10.3
– net interest	480.00	10.2
Dividends from share investments		
– gross	1,500.00	10.17
– tax credit	150.00	10.16
– dividends	1,350.00	10.15
(5) Reliefs		
In the year George paid £312 (equivalent		
to £400 before tax) under Gift Aid to		
the Cancer Research Campaign		15A.1

George applied for, and was granted, permission to defer payment of Class 4 National Insurance Contributions.

Tax payments of £1,300 have been made on both 31 January 2007 and 31 July 2007 based on George's tax liability for 2005/06.

Unfortunately, HMRC's Tax Calculation Guide runs to a substantial number of pages and there is insufficient space to reproduce them here. An abbreviated version of George Salmon's tax calculation is as follows:

	£	£
Employment		
Salary and taxable benefits	45,580	
Less: Professional subscription	100	
		45,480
Self-employment		10,000
UK interest (before tax)		
Interest from UK building society	600	
National Savings interest paid gross	250	
		850
UK dividends and tax credits		1,500
Total income		**57,830**
Deductions for:		
Self-employed contributions to personal pension plans		2,500
Gift Aid payment		400
Total deductions		2,900
Total income less deductions		54,930
Allowances given as deduction from income:		
Personal allowance		5,035
Net Income Chargeable to Tax		49,895
Tax thereon:		
Non-savings income at starting rate, £2,150 at 10%		215.00
Non-savings income at basic rate, £31,150 at 22%		6,853.00
Non-savings income at higher rate, £14,245 at 40%		5,698.00
Savings income (excluding dividends) at higher savings rate, £850 at 40%		340.00
Dividends at higher dividend rate, £1,500 at 32.5%		487.50
		13,593.50

Allowances and reliefs given in terms of tax:

Non-repayable tax credits on dividends	(150.00)
Income Tax due after allowances and reliefs	13,443.50
Recoverable tax on Gift Aid payment	88.00
Tax deducted at source from personal pension premiums	550.00
Income Tax	14,081.50
Tax paid at source:	
On salary	(9,926.00)
On UK savings	(120.00)
Income Tax due for 2006/07	**4,035.50**

TAX PAYMENTS

Tax due for 2006/07 (as above)	4,035.50
Payment on account made 31 January 2007	(1,300.00)
Payment on account made 31 July 2007	(1,300.00)
Balance due for 2006/07	**1,435.50**
Add: First payment on account for 2007/08	2,017.75
Amount due on 31 January 2008	**3,453.25**
Second payment on account for 2007/08	2,017.75
Amount due on 31 July 2008	**2,017.75**

From his tax calculation George will then be able to fill in question 18 of his Tax Return as follows:

Q18	Do you want to calculate your tax and, if appropriate, Class 4 National Insurance contributions and Student Loan Repayment?	YES ✓	Use your Tax Calculation Guide then fill in boxes 18.1 to 18.8 as appropriate.
•	Underpaid tax for earlier years included in your tax code for 2006-07	18.1 £	
•	Underpaid tax for 2006–07 included in your tax code for 2007–08	18.2 £	
•	Student Loan Repayment due	18.2A £	
•	Class 4 NICs due	18.2B £	
•	Pension charges due - *enter the amount from box 32 of the Pensions supplementary Page*	18.2C £	
•	Total tax, Class 4 NICs and Student Loan Repayment due for 2006–07 **before** you made any payments on account *(put the amount in brackets if an overpayment.)*	18.3 £ *4,035-50*	
•	Tax due calculated by reference to earlier years - *see the notes on page 10 of your Tax Calculation Guide (SA151W).*	18.4 £	
•	Reduction in tax due calculated by reference to earlier years - *see the notes on page 10 of your Tax Calculation Guide (SA151W).*	18.5 £	
•	Tick box 18.6 if you are claiming to reduce your 2007–08 payments on account. Make sure you enter the **reduced** amount of your first payment in box 18.7. Then, in the 'Additional information' box, box 23.9 on page 10, say why you are making a claim	18.6	
•	Your first payment on account for 2007–08 *(please include the pence.)*	18.7 £	
•	Any 2007–08 tax you are reclaiming now	18.8 £ *2,017-75*	

HMRC 12/06   TAX RETURN: PAGE 7   *Please turn over* ▶

What HMRC does

When your completed Tax Return is received by your tax office it will be processed as quickly as possible based on your figures. Any simple mistakes will be corrected right away and you will be told about them. This may simply be because your figures do not add up.

If you want to claim a repayment because you have paid too much tax you should answer 'Yes' to Q19. You can, if you want, nominate a charity to receive all or part of your repayment. To do so you will need to answer Q19A appropriately. Information on how to go about this can be found on page 29 of your Tax Return Guide. But if you want to receive your tax repayment personally tick 'Yes' to Q19B and provide the information requested.

You will be sent a calculation of your tax position if you have asked HMRC to do it for you. If you have worked out your own tax bill, and it is wrong, you will also be advised of the mistakes you have made.

Once your Tax Return has been processed it will be checked. HMRC have 12 months from 31 January 2008 to check your Tax Return for the year ended 5 April 2007 (longer if you are late in submitting your Return). Remember that enquiries may be made into your figures and you may be asked by your tax office to send in your records in support of them.

Online filing

This is something that will come to us all one day and it saves HMRC (and, therefore, taxpayers in general) time and money. The difference in reality is that the Return is filed by the touch of a button rather than the lick of a stamp.

In order to use this service you will need to register with the government gateway, a link to which can be found on the HMRC Home Page www.hmrc.gov.uk. You will need to give your Unique Taxpayer Reference (UTR) together with your National Insurance Number and/or Postcode. Within seven days a user name and activation PIN will be sent to you by post, allowing you access to your own area within the HMRC website. Here, you will also be able to view your statement of account showing the amount you owe, or are due back from, your accounts office.

In order to complete your Tax Return you will need to choose your software from a selection of authorised software houses. Alternatively you can use HMRC's own software. Once downloaded, and in some cases paid for, you are ready to begin work.

Depending on the software chosen the form is completed either directly, as you would the paper version, or via a question and answer session. Some software allows both methods and others build in rather useful checking routines.

15 PAYING YOUR TAX, INTEREST, SURCHARGES AND PENALTIES

Under the Self-Assessment tax system:

- there are specified dates each year when you must pay your tax;

- you regularly receive a Statement of Account from HMRC detailing both tax recently paid and the next amount due.

Tax payment dates

The tax payment dates for 2006/07 are:

	Due Date for Tax Payments on Account	Due Date for Final Balance
Rental income and untaxed investment income		
Business profits	50% 31/01/2007	31/01/2008
Unpaid PAYE (where not coded)	50% 31/07/2007	
Higher Rate Tax on investment income (taxed at source)		
Capital Gains Tax	N/A	31/01/2008

The one exception to the rule requiring direct payment of tax to HMRC relates to employees or pensioners who send in their Tax Returns to their Tax Office by no later than 30 September following the end of the tax year. If they owe less than £2,000 in tax they can choose to have the amount collected monthly in the following year through the PAYE system.

Payments on account

As the table on the left shows, some taxpayers, who will mainly be the self-employed, will make two payments on account of the tax due for a year on:

- 31 January in the tax year; and

- 31 July following the end of the tax year.

Payments on account are worked out by splitting into two equal amounts the tax paid for the previous tax year (after taking off tax incurred at source and any Capital Gains Tax).

You do not need to make payments on account of Income Tax if:

- the amount you owe for Income Tax and Class 4 National Insurance Contributions for the previous tax year – after taking off tax paid at source on, for example, dividends, bank and building society interest – is less than £500; or

- at least 80% of your Income Tax and Class 4 National Insurance Contributions bill for the preceding tax year was represented by tax deducted from the income before you received it.

It follows that most employees and pensioners will not have to make the half-yearly payments on account.

Reduced payments on account

Maybe, because of a change in your financial circumstances, your payments on account for the tax year (based on what you paid in the previous year) point towards an overstatement of your likely liability for the year.

This might happen where you expect:

- your income in 2007/08 to be lower than that in 2006/07;

- your allowances or reliefs to be higher;

- that more of your income will incur tax at source in 2007/08, because:

  — it will be taxed under PAYE; or

  — your savings income taxed at source will increase.

In such circumstances you can claim to reduce your payments on account. You do this by using Form SA303, which is available at your Tax Office. The form gives guidance on how to complete it. When you have done this and signed it you should send it back to your Tax Office for processing.

If the claim to reduce your payments on account subsequently turns out to be excessive then you will be asked to pay interest on the difference between the reduced tax you actually paid and the payments on account that should have been made.

Statements of account

The main features of the statements sent to taxpayers showing their account with HMRC are:

- an opening balance, if any, brought forward from the previous statement;

- what has happened since the last statement;

- whether there is an over payment or, most probably, an amount to pay, and when to pay it.

If you are making payments on account you can expect to receive the following statements up to February 2008:

July 2007	**To tell you of the second payment on account for 2006/07 due on 31 July 2007.**
August 2007	**To let you know of any outstanding balance of the second payment on account. The statement will also include a figure for interest due to date.**
January 2008	**To advise you of your balancing payment for 2006/07 and your first payment on account for 2007/08, both due on 31 January 2008.**
February 2008	**To show any outstanding amounts which should have been paid on 31 January 2008. The statement will also include a charge for interest due to date.**

You will also receive statements of account:

- whenever they are amended;

- every month where there is an outstanding amount in excess of £500;

- every two months where you still owe tax of between £32 and £500; and

- where you are due a refund from HMRC (but only once!).

Other points of interest are:

- As HMRC carry out security checks any tax refund due to you may not actually be issued until sometime after the date shown on your Statement of Account.

- Where a tax liability will shortly be due for payment HMRC will usually set any tax refund against this amount and then just repay the balance.

- If you have made a payment in the short period before you receive a Statement it will appear on the next one.

If you have registered for Self-Assessment Online you can access a wide range of services to include:

- Viewing the latest issued copy of your Statement, as well as any Statements issued to you in the last three years.

- Viewing payments/credits and how these have been allocated.

- Viewing liabilities by tax year including interest, penalties and surcharges.

- Requesting repayments where an account is in credit.

- Claiming to reduce payments on account.

- Viewing and changing your address.

- Paying online.

Paying your tax

There are a number of secure and efficient methods for paying your tax recommended by HMRC. If you use payment by post you should make your cheque payable to 'H.M. Revenue and Customs only' followed by your Unique Taxpayer Reference. Your cheque should be accompanied by the tear-off payment slip from your statement of account and both of these should be sent, unfolded, to your Accounts Office in the envelope provided.

HMRC politely requests that:

- you do not staple or attach paperclips to cheques; and

- you do not pay your tax by sending cash through the post.

You can assist your Accounts Office in dealing promptly with your tax payment by:

- including a separate letter if you are sending a post-dated cheque, or want to give further information about your payment; and

- paying on time – you will not then incur interest charges.

You can also pay:

- using the Internet or telephone;

- at a post office or your bank; or

- by debit card (Switch, Solo, Electron or Visa Delta) over the Internet.

Certificates of tax deposit

You can provide for the payment of a future tax liability by purchasing a Certificate of Tax Deposit. The main features of such certificates are:

- the minimum value is £500;

- they earn interest from the date of purchase to the normal due date for payment of the tax; and

- the interest is taxable.

Date of receipt

Tax payments are considered to be received by your Accounts Office as follows:

Payment Method	Effective Date of Payment
Handed in at an HMRC office or received by post (except below)	day of receipt by HMRC
Received by post following a day when the office has been closed for whatever reason (including a weekend)	the day the office was first closed (for payments received on Monday, the effective date will be the previous Saturday)

Electronic Funds Transfer (EFT) – payment by BACS or CHAPS (Clearing House Automated Payment System)	**one working day immediately before the date that the value is received. (A working day is defined as a Bank of England working day.)**
Bank Giro or Girobank	**three working days before the date of processing by HMRC**

Interest

You will be charged interest if you are late in paying your tax. At the time of going to print the annual interest rate is 7.5% and is calculated from the due date up until payment of the tax. Tax relief on the interest is not allowed.

There may be circumstances when the imposition of interest would not be fair to you and can be justifiably contested. HMRC's Code of Practice entitled 'Mistakes by HMRC' points out that an Inspector will waive interest where delays have occurred for more than six months over and above the twenty-eight-day target for dealing with such matters. The booklet goes on to say:

'If there is no good reason for a delay, and we have taken more than six months in total – over and above the twenty-eight-day target we have set ourselves – we will, for amounts unpaid, or not repaid, because of our delay:

- give up interest that arose on unpaid tax during the period of our delay; or

- pay you interest (called "repayment interest") on money we owed you during the period of our delay; and

- pay any reasonable costs which you have incurred as a direct result of our delay.'

You will be paid interest, which is called repayment supplement and is not taxable, by HMRC on overpayment of any of the following:

- payments on account of Income Tax;

- Income tax and Capital Gains Tax;

- surcharges on late payment of tax;

- any penalties imposed.

At the time of going to print the annual rate of repayment supplement is 3.00%.

Remission of tax

Arrears of Income Tax or Capital Gains Tax may be waived if they result from HMRC's failure to make proper and timely use of information supplied by:

- the taxpayer about his or her own income, capital gains or personal circumstances;

- an employer, where the information affects an employee's notice of coding; or

- the DWP about a taxpayer's retirement, disability or widow's State Pension.

The concession is normally only given where the taxpayer:

- could reasonably have believed that his or her tax affairs were in order; and

- is notified of the arrears by the end of the tax year following that in which it arose.

Surcharges

Surcharges are levied on late payment of Income Tax, but not payments on account, or Capital Gains Tax as follows:

Tax unpaid by 28 February (one month after the tax was due)	**5% of unpaid tax**
Tax unpaid by 31 July (six months after the tax was due)	**Further 5% of tax unpaid**

A surcharge notice must be formally served on you by HMRC. You have 30 days in which to appeal against the notice if you think you have a reasonable excuse for late payment of the tax. Your appeal might be successful:

- if there is clear evidence that your cheque was lost in the post; or

- in the event of serious illness.

Examples of circumstances where your appeal will be rejected are:

- cheques wrongly made out; and

- lack of funds other than for exceptional reasons.

Penalties

The main penalties under Self-Assessment are:

Offence	Penalty
You do not submit your Tax Return to your Tax Office by 31 January after the end of the tax year	£100
Your Return is still outstanding after a further six months	Further £100

These penalties will be reduced to the amount of tax owing where this is less than £100.

Where taxpayers have a genuinely good excuse for missing the annual 31 January deadline for submitting Tax Returns they can appeal against the automatic late filing penalty.

What may be accepted by HMRC as a reasonable excuse for late filing include:

- where the Tax Return was not received by the taxpayer;

- where the Tax Return was lost in the post or delayed because of:

  — fire or flood at the post office where the Tax Return was handled;

  — prolonged industrial action within the post office;

  — an unforeseen event which disrupted the postal services;

- where a taxpayer lost his or her tax records as a result of fire, flood or theft;

- serious illness;

- death of a spouse, domestic partner or close relative.

HMRC will not agree the following as a reasonable excuse for being late:

- Tax Return too difficult;

- pressure of work;

- lack of information; or
- absence of reminders from HMRC.

The other penalties are:

Offence	*Penalty*
Late returns	Up to £60 per day extra on application to the Commissioners by HMRC
Returns still outstanding after the anniversary of the filing date	£200 and a further sum up to the amount of the tax payable
You do not receive a Tax Return and fail to notify HMRC of chargeability to tax within six months of the end of the tax year	Not exceeding the tax due
Fraudulently or negligently delivering an incorrect Tax Return	Up to the amount of the difference between the tax actually payable and that which was shown as due
Not notifying HMRC that you have started up in business within three months after the end of the month in which you commenced your self-employment	£100
Failure to produce documents during an HMRC enquiry	An initial penalty of £50 followed by a further penalty of up to £30 for each day during which the failure continues
Failure to maintain and keep records	Up to £3,000
Fraudulently or negligently claiming to reduce interim tax payments	Up to an amount equivalent to the difference between the tax paid and the tax that should have been paid

Generally a penalty determination must be made, or proceedings commence, within six years of the date on which the penalty was incurred. The Rules allow for this period of time to be extended to any later date within three years of the final determination of the tax liability.

16 ELECTIONS AND CLAIMS – TIME LIMITS

You will already have gathered that certain options available to you as a taxpayer are dependent on you submitting an election or claim to HMRC. As these will usually involve a saving in tax it is important to appreciate that you often need to act within prescribed time limits. This chapter brings together those elections and claims that are most likely to concern you. It also sets out the time available during which they must be submitted to HMRC. It is by no means exhaustive.

Chapter 2 – Tax Rates and Allowances

Election/Claim	*Time Limit*
The various elections for the transfer of the married couple's and blind person's allowances	Generally before the start of the tax year for which it is to have effect
Claim to the personal allowances detailed in the chapter	No later than five years after 31 January next following the end of the tax year
Transfer of excess allowances between husband and wife	No later than five years after 31 January next following the end of the tax year

Chapter 3 – Tax Credits

Claims for Tax Credits	Claims will only be backdated by a maximum of three months

Chapter 6 – Value Added Tax

Election/Claim	*Time Limit*
Application for Registration	No later than 30 days from the end of the month after the one when turnover exceeds the registration limit
Claim for Bad Debt Relief	When a debt remains unpaid for more than six months

Chapter 7 – Working for Yourself

Election/Claim	*Time Limit*
Relief for post-cessation expenses	No later than one year after 31 January next following the tax year in which the payments are made
Creating a separate pool to work out the capital allowances on an asset with a short life expectancy	No later than one year after 31 January next following the tax year in which the period of account ended in which the expenditure is incurred
Relief for the loss sustained in the the tax year against other income of the same year or the preceding year	Within one year after 31 January next following the tax year in which the loss arose
Relief for a trading loss against the profits arising from the same trade in subsequent periods	Within five years after 31 January next following the tax year in which the loss was sustained
Relief for the loss in the first four years of assessment of a new business to be given against the income of the three preceding years of assessment	No later than one year after 31 January next following the tax year in which the loss occurred
Relief for trading losses to be offset against capital gains	No later than one year after 31 January next following the tax year
Relief for the loss in the last 12 months of trading to be given against the profits of the same trade which were assessed in the three tax years prior to the year in which the trade was discontinued	Within five years after 31 January next following the tax year in which the trade ceased

Chapter 10 – Savings and Investment Income

Election/Claim	*Time Limit*
An election to opt out of Rent-a-Room relief for a particular tax year, or withdrawal of an election	Within one year after 31 January next following the tax year

An election for the alternative basis of Rent-a-Room relief, or revocation of an election	Within one year after 31 January next following the tax year
Claim for Income Tax relief under the Enterprise Investment Scheme	Within five years after 31 January next following that in which the shares were issued
Declaration by a married couple or civil partners that their beneficial interest in joint property and the income arising from it are unequal	The date of the declaration which must be sent to HMRC within 60 days

Chapter 13 – Capital Gains

Election/Claim	*Time Limit*
Claim to the capital loss where the value of an asset becomes negligible	The loss arises on the date of claim although, in practice, a two-year period is allowed from the end of the tax year in which the asset became of negligible value
Claim for the loss on shares that were originally subscribed for in an unquoted trading company to be set against income in the year of loss, or the preceding year	No later than one year after 31 January next following the tax year in which the loss was made
An election for the capital gains on disposals of assets you owned on 31 March 1982 to be worked out by reference to their values on that date, ignoring original costs	Within one year after 31 January next following the tax year in which the first disposal of an asset you owned on 31 March 1982 takes place
Claim for the 6 April 1965 value to be substituted in a calculation of the capital gain arising on the sale of an asset held at that date	No later than one year after 31 January next following the tax year in which the disposal is made
An election to determine which of your homes is to be regarded as your principal residence for Capital Gains Tax purposes	Two years from the date when two or more properties are eligible

17   INHERITANCE TAX

Not only might Inheritance Tax be payable on transfers or gifts you make during your lifetime, but it is also due on the value of your estate on death. Husband and wife are treated as separate individuals, and both are entitled to the various exemptions. Inheritance Tax is far from straightforward. What follows is a brief outline. The Tax is administered by the Capital Taxes Office, to whom all Returns and Accounts should be submitted.

Potentially exempt transfers

The most significant feature of Inheritance Tax is the concept of a potentially exempt transfer (PET). This is:

- an outright gift to an individual; or

- a gift into a settlement for the benefit of a disabled person.

No tax is payable provided the donor lives for at least seven years after making the gift. A form of tapering relief applies where death occurs within seven years. The amount of Inheritance Tax is then calculated at the rates that apply at the date of death as shown in the following table:

Number of Years between Gift and Death	% of Tax Payable
Not more than 3	100
Between 3 and 4	80
Between 4 and 5	60
Between 5 and 6	40
Between 6 and 7	20

Suppose, however, the PET is within the limit of chargeable transfers taxable at a nil rate. There will then be no benefit from tapering relief as no Inheritance Tax is payable on the PET.

Gifts with reservation and Pre-Owned Assets

If you make a gift but continue to enjoy some benefit from it, the property or asset you have given away is likely to be treated as yours until either the date when you cease to enjoy any benefit from the gift, or your death. This is a 'gift with reservation'. For example, you give your house to your children but continue to live there, rent free. Your house would then be counted as part of your estate and the seven-year period would not start until you either moved home or began to pay a commercial rent.

You are also chargeable to income tax each year on the benefit of the continuing and free use of any assets that you have given away.

Lifetime gifts

If you make a lifetime gift which is not a potentially exempt transfer:

- The excess, if any, over the nil rate band will attract liability to Inheritance Tax.

- The rate of tax payable is one half of the rates that apply on death.

An example of such a lifetime gift is a transfer into most types of Trust.

Exemptions

The main exemptions applicable to individuals are:

- transfers between husband and wife, during lifetime and on death;

- similarly between civil partners;

- gifts up to £3,000 in any one tax year. Any part of the exemption that is left over can be carried forward to the following year only. For example, if your total transfers came to £1,200 during 2005/06 you could have given away as much as £4,800 during 2006/07 all within your annual exemption limit. However, if your gifts totalled £3,000 in 2005/06, you would be limited to £3,000 in 2006/07 as well;

- gifts to any one person up to £250 per person in each tax year. Where the total amount given to any one individual exceeds this limit no part comes within this exemption; and

- marriage gifts. The amount you can give away in consideration of marriage depends on your relationship to the bride or groom, as follows:

	£
By either parent	5,000
By a grandparent or great-grandparent	2,500
By any other person	1,000

- regular gifts out of income which form part of your normal expenditure;

- gifts to charities and 'qualifying' political parties, both without limit. Both these exceptions apply to lifetime gifts and to bequests on death.

Business property

Subject to certain conditions, qualifying business assets and interests in businesses qualify for relief for transfers arising either in lifetime or on death. There are two rates:

100% for:

- unincorporated businesses;

- all holdings of unquoted shares in qualifying companies.

Unquoted shares include those traded on the AIM and PLUS markets.

50% for:

- shares giving control of a quoted company;

- land, buildings, machinery or plant used in a partnership or controlled company where the transferor is a partner or controlling shareholder.

Agricultural property

The reliefs applying to agricultural land and holdings are similar to those for business property. Subject to certain minimum ownership and use conditions, the two rates are again:

100% for:

- land and buildings where the transferor has vacant possession, or the right to obtain it, within 12 months;
- agricultural property let for periods exceeding 12 months where the letting commenced on or after 1 September 1995.

50% for:

- other qualifying property.

Rates of tax

Each taxable gift or transfer is not considered in isolation in calculating how much tax is payable on it. In working out how much is payable, previous taxable transfers are taken into account. This is because the tax due on each chargeable gift or the value of your estate on death is dependent upon the cumulative value of all other chargeable transfers in the seven years leading up to the date of the next chargeable transfer. The rates payable on death from 6 April 2006 are:

Band (£)	Rate %
0–285,000	0
Over 285,000	40

These rates also apply to all lifetime gifts or transfers within three years of death. Inheritance Tax payable on PETS more than three years before but within seven years of death is determined by the first table in this chapter.

Death

When somebody dies, their assets pass to their estate. The estate is then administered by their personal representatives, whose main duties are to:

- gather in the assets left by the deceased individual;
- settle their debts;
- pay out any legacies; and then
- distribute any remaining assets to the beneficiaries.

On a death an Inheritance Tax Return form is completed and submitted together with an application for a Grant of:

- probate where there is a will; or

- administration where there is no will.

The Return must be lodged within 12 months of the date of death. It must include information about previous transfers and gifts which are required to work out the amount of Inheritance Tax payable. Therefore, you are well advised to maintain complete records of your lifetime gifts. Also, to help your executors you should maintain up-to-date details of all your assets and where the supporting certificates and documents are stored.

Usually it is not necessary to submit a Return where the deceased's estate does not exceed £240,000.

As with your annual Tax Return there are penalties for late Returns, delays, negligence or fraud.

Wendy Brown, a widow, died on 30 September 2006 leaving her entire estate to her daughter. She did not make any gifts in the seven years leading up to her death. Her assets and unpaid bills on her death were:

Assets	Value	
	£	£
Flat	220,000	
Household effects	2,000	
Car	5,000	
Building society account	30,000	
Shares	40,000	
Current account	2,500	
		299,500
Less: *Allowable Deductions*		
Funeral expenses	920	
Income Tax	500	
Telephone bill	50	
Electricity bill	60	
		1,530
Net Value of Estate		£297,970

Inheritance Tax Payable

On first £285,000	Nil
On next £12,970 at 40%	£5,188
	£5,188

The tax is payable out of Wendy Brown's estate by the executors of her will.

Sales at a loss

Relief is available where certain assets are sold during specified periods after death for less than the valuation at the date of death.

- In the case of land and buildings, the period is four years.

- For quoted securities the time limit is one year.

The relief is available to 'the appropriate person' (the one who pays the tax). All sales by that person in the respective periods must be aggregated. As a result, losses may accordingly be reduced or eliminated by profits so that the relief could be restricted or lost. When this type of relief is due, the net proceeds of sale are substituted for the valuation at death. The Inheritance Tax liability is then recalculated.

Payment of tax

The persons primarily liable for payment of Inheritance Tax are:

- the transferor in respect of chargeable lifetime gifts;

- the personal representatives on death.

There is a process that allows personal representatives to draw on funds held in a deceased's bank and building society accounts solely for the purpose of paying any Inheritance Tax that is due before the Grant of Probate can be issued.

The due dates for payment are:

- for chargeable lifetime gifts – six months after the end of the month in which the gift was made; or

- for potentially exempt transfers which become chargeable on death, and the charge on death itself – six months after the end of the month in which the death occurred.

There is an option to pay the tax on certain types of asset by ten equal annual instalments. The first payment is due on the normal due date.

The relevant assets are:

- land and buildings;

- controlling shareholdings;

- unquoted shares, subject to certain conditions; and

- businesses.

In the case of lifetime transfers which are, or become, chargeable, the instalment option is only available if the tax is borne by the transferee. Where the asset is sold during the instalment paying period, outstanding instalments become payable immediately.

Interest is payable on Inheritance Tax liabilities from the due date until the date of payment. At the time of going to print the rate of interest is 4%. Where the instalment option is in force, no interest is payable on the outstanding instalments except on:

- land and buildings which do not qualify for business property or agricultural property relief; and

- shares and securities in investment companies.

Intestacy

If you die without having made a will your estate will be divided up under the statutory intestacy rules. If you are married and survived by both your spouse and children, your spouse is entitled to a statutory legacy of £125,000. This increases to £200,000 if there are no children but you are survived by specific relatives.

The present intestacy rules for individuals who die domiciled in England or Wales can be summarized as follows:

Unmarried individual

Survived by

Children or grandchildren	The total estate is shared in the
Parents	following order of priority,
Brothers and sisters	to the exclusion of all others.
Half-brothers and half-sisters	
Grandparents	
Uncles and aunts	
The Crown	

Married individual

Particular Circumstances		*Division*
(1)	Estate amounts to less than £125,000	All to spouse
(2)	Estate exceeds £125,000 and there are children	Spouse is entitled to first £125,000 and a life interest in half the remainder. The balance is shared between the children
(3)	Estate is worth less than £200,000 and there are no children	All to spouse
(4)	Estate comes to more than £200,000, the couple have no children but parents are still alive	Spouse receives first £200,000 and half the remainder absolutely. The parents divide the rest
(5)	As in (4) above, parents are dead, but there are brothers and sisters	As in (4) above but the balance is shared between the brothers and sisters instead of the parents
(6)	The only survivor is the spouse	All to spouse

The spouse must survive the intestate individual by 28 days to become entitled under the intestacy rules.

Civil partners, and the children of a civil partnership, benefit under the intestacy rules in the same way as spouses and the children of a marriage.

In Scotland the intestacy rules have no application to estates of individuals who die domiciled there. Furthermore, a surviving spouse and/or children are entitled to fixed proportions of the moveable estate of the deceased individual. This rule applies whether the deceased died intestate or had made a will.

Legacies

Any Inheritance Tax due on a legacy you receive under a will will be accounted for by the executors of the estate before the legacy is paid over to you. You do not pay either Income Tax or Capital Gains Tax on a legacy. It does not need to be reported on your annual Tax Return.

18   TAX-SAVING POINTERS

Throughout all the stages of life, from the time we are born until the day we die, decisions need to be taken on our tax and financial affairs. During our years of minority these are dealt with by our parents. When we reach adulthood at age 18, which is about the time we leave school and head for university, we become responsible for everything in life including tax and dealing with HMRC. After university comes a life of work, most likely for someone else, but maybe for ourselves in self-employment. In this period of the cycle of life we:

- Are likely to get married or enter a civil partnership.

- May buy our own home.

- Will want to save through a pension and make investments to provide for the day when we retire.

Our years in retirement:

- are most likely to be those when we will need to maximise our income from pensions and savings; and

- are probably those when we will concentrate on doing what we can to minimise the amount of our estates that goes on death duties – Inheritance Tax.

At every stage it is important to make well-informed decisions to ensure that we follow the best strategies for achieving our goals. When it comes to tax:

- we may need to adjust our finances to take account of future reductions or increases in the various taxes;

- we should not consider saving tax without having due regard to other criteria; and

- we should always be ready to respond to any shift in tax policy following a change in Government.

I like to think that somewhere in the following sections you will find pointers to help you save on tax.

Childhood and Teenage Years

- Do not miss out on collecting your Child Benefit. It does not depend on income and is tax-free.

- Make sure you receive the £250 voucher so you can open a Child Trust Fund account for your new baby. Family and friends can add up to £1,200 each year to the Fund.

- If you are on a low or modest income you should be able to claim the Child Tax Credit. Do not delay in making your claim since it can only be backdated for a maximum of 3 months.

- Children's Bonus Bonds, issued by National Savings and Investments, are totally tax-free and particularly suitable for investing gifts from parents.

- Like any other taxpayer children and teenagers are allowed income of £5,035 for 2006/07 before paying tax.

Tax Compliance

- First and foremost, keep proper and orderly records. This will make it easier for you to complete your Tax Return fully and accurately. Furthermore, if your tax office decides to enquire into your Tax Return the records you have maintained will enable you to demonstrate that the Return is both accurate and complete.

- Also remember to keep your records for the right length of time. This is much longer if you are self-employed or letting property.

- Make sure you fill in your Tax Return properly by only writing in the spaces provided using blue or black ink and using numbers, without pence, when asked for amounts.

- If the amount of any of your sources of income is substantially different compared to the previous year, use the additional information box on page 10 to explain the reason for the change.

- Always answer "yes" to question 19 on page 8 of your Tax Return. Any tax overpaid plus tax-free interest on the repayment will then be refunded to you. Otherwise it is likely that the overpayment will be kept by HMRC to be set-off against a future tax liability.

- Remember that you can amend your self-assessment at any time in the 12 month period after the latest 31 January filing deadline.

- Do not forget to sign the Return. This is one of the most common mistakes that HMRC have found when processing Tax Returns. Others include failing to complete the self-employed pages and a separate supplementary page for each individual employment.

- Make your charitable donations under the Gift Aid Scheme. The tax you deduct and retain at the basic rate will then be refunded by HMRC to your chosen charities. Furthermore, if you are a top-rate taxpayer, you will also gain as you can deduct the grossed up equivalent of your donations under Gift Aid in working out how much tax you pay at the 40% rate.

- But if you give assets, instead of cash, to a charity you can save on both Income Tax and Capital Gains Tax

- Remember the key dates in the self-assessment calendar which are summarised in Appendix 10 at the end of the book.

- Of particular importance are the two dates for sending back your Tax Return each year. These are 30 September and 31 January after the end of the tax year. You must send your Return back by 30 September if you want HMRC to work out your tax bill.

- The same 30 September deadline applies if you pay tax under PAYE, and want any tax underpayment of less than £2,000 collected by an adjustment to your PAYE code in the following year.

- Do not forget that the second send-back date of 31 January is critical. You must stick to it otherwise you will be charged a fixed £100 penalty for the late Return.

- Always pay your tax on time. If you are late in making payment then not only will you be charged interest but you will also run the risk of incurring a surcharge.

In Employment

- Contributions made by your employer to a company pension scheme in which you participate or into your own personal pension plan are not taxable on you.

- There are not many employment related expenses on which you can claim tax relief but you are allowed tax relief on subscriptions to a professional body and on the cost of clothing and upkeep of tools in most classes of industry as set out in Appendix 2.

- Find out whether your employer operates one of the various share, profit-sharing and share option, schemes all of which have different investment limits and levels of tax relief. Membership of whatever scheme is on offer may be an attractive long-term investment with built-in tax advantages.

- For many employees the company car continues to be an important part of the remuneration package. The system of taxing company cars is geared towards encouraging the cleaner use of cars by linking the tax charge to the exhaust emission of the car. When the time comes for you to change your company car it will pay you to look into the carbon dioxide emission of the proposed replacement car. You will save tax on your company car benefit by opting for a car with a lower approved CO_2 emission figure.

- The cost of petrol or diesel for your private mileage paid by your employer is a taxable benefit worked out on the CO_2 emission figure for your car. You will often be better off paying for your own fuel for non-business travel.

- Sometimes it is better to own your own car and charge your employer for the cost of all your business mileage but you must keep a proper and detailed log of all business and private mileage.

- If your employer pays you a mileage allowance for using your car, motorcycle or bicycle for business you can claim tax relief on any difference between the amount you receive and the statutory rate.

- Remember that there is no tax charge on parking spaces provided at, or near, your workplace.

- Around January/February each year look out for your new PAYE Coding Notice for the following tax year. Make sure you have been given the right allowances and that any deductions for unpaid tax or benefits-in-kind are correct. Get in touch with your Tax Office if anything is not right.

- Check that you have not overpaid on National Insurance contributions. This is likely to happen if you have more than one job, or you are in work and self-employed at the same time. Excess contributions can be reclaimed from HMRC after the end of the tax year.

Working for Yourself – Tax

- Do not forget to advise HMRC as soon as you begin self-employment. There is a £100 penalty if you do not let them know within 3 months of commencement.

- Then think about your accounting date. 31 March is an obvious and convenient choice as the date coincides with the end of the tax year on 5 April. However, it is sometimes preferable to go with a date early on in the tax year, such as 30 April, as it allows you more time to plan for the funding of the tax payable.

- Alternatively, if your business is seasonal in nature, it may be a good idea to pick an annual accounting date to coincide with the slack time of the year and when stocks are low.

- Maintain proper accounting records for your business. Make sure they are accurate and always up-to-date.

- Avoid using estimates for some business expenses. If they are challenged on enquiry by HMRC you will find it difficult to substantiate the claim in your accounts.

- Where you incur mixed expenses – part business with the balance private – be careful over the apportionment calculation and only claim the proper and reasonable business element as an expense for tax purposes.

- Maybe you need to buy some plant and machinery or, for example, a new car, for your business. It may be tax efficient to do so towards the end of the current accounting year rather than early on in the following year. You will benefit from the capital allowances due on the expenditure at an earlier date.

- Where appropriate pay your spouse or partner a fair and justifiable salary for secretarial or other assistance given to you.

- Consider taking your spouse/partner into partnership where he or she helps you in the business and your annual profits are such that the top slice is taxable at the higher 40% rate. Between you it may be possible to make significant savings in your overall annual tax bill.

- Explore all the different options available for claiming the tax relief due on a business loss. You may well find that one or other of the alternative types of loss/relief claim produces a bigger tax repayment. In doing your calculations take into account the amount of the tax-free repayment supplement which would be paid by HMRC.

- Make sure you claim your entitlement to the Small Business Rate Relief. This allows small businesses a reduction of up to 50% of their full charge for rates. The deadline for claims for 2006/07 is 30 September 2007.

- If your business is booming and is extremely profitable you should seriously think about transferring it to a Limited company where you own the shares. You may well be able to reduce your overall tax burden but it is an area where you should seek advice from a tax specialist.

- Finally, always look to the future and plan for your retirement whether you be contemplating a sale of your business or handing it down to the next generation.

Working for Yourself – Value Added Tax

- If your business is not within VAT, plan ahead so you know when to register. Then maintain a regular check on your turnover to make sure you are not exceeding the limit for registration.

- Sometimes it pays to apply for voluntary registration. You may be able to reclaim significant amounts of VAT on purchases for, and expenses of your business. However, it is worth checking on your customers to make sure that they are VAT registered and will be able to recover the VAT charged on your invoices.

- Make sure you submit each VAT Return and pay what is due to HMRC within the stipulated time limit.

- If the annual turnover of your business is under £150,000 perhaps the Flat Rate Scheme is for you. It will save you time in dealing with the requirements of normal accounting for VAT.

- Look into the respective merits of the Annual or Cash Accounting Schemes. They each have different turnover limits for you to be able to participate in them.

- Always speak up if things go wrong or if there is something you do not understand. HMRC generally want to help you get things right. Always give the full facts and quote your VAT number.

Income from Savings

- Non-taxpayers (such as some pensioners, children or dependent married spouses) should get the special form so they can apply to receive their bank and building society interest without any deduction for tax. This will save them having to claim a tax refund from HMRC.

- Married couples and civil partners should look to see whether they need to transfer their income producing assets between them in order to maximise their entitlement to personal allowances and, where applicable, the starting and/or savings and basic rate tax bands. If, for some reason, this is inappropriate, joint ownership might be an alternative.

- Individuals in the top 40% tax bracket should take a look at those investments available from National Savings and Investments where the return is free of both Income Tax and Capital Gains Tax.

- If you are contemplating the purchase of a property which you are then going to let out as an investment it may well pay you to take out a loan to assist in financing the purchase. You will be able to claim the annual interest on the borrowing as a deduction from the net rental income of the property.

- Properties let out as Furnished Holiday Accommodation qualify for many tax concessions, including income tax relief on losses from running the business.

- Alternatively remortgage your buy to let property releasing funds for other uses and still get tax relief on the interest.

- If you are a landlord don't overlook the one-off allowance of up to £1,500 per property on energy saving insulation available on expenditure up to 5 April 2009. This covers wall, loft and hot-water systems.

- Make sure your ISA is the right account for you. If you want to invest more than £4,000 in stocks and shares in any one tax year, you must open a MAXI ISA. You can only contribute to one MAXI ISA each tax year. In the same tax year you cannot subscribe to both a MINI and a MAXI ISA although you can contribute to two separate MINI ISAs investing in each of the two different types of investment (stocks and shares and cash). You are not allowed to subscribe to more than one MINI ISA investing in the same type of investment in each tax year.

- You do not have to terminate any PEPs you still hold although you cannot add any new money to them. They can continue under the present rules, free of tax on both income and capital gains.

- You can withdraw up to 5% per annum tax-free each year from a non-qualifying life policy such as a single premium investment bond. This could be a good way to supplement your income, particularly for a 40% taxpayer.

- Venture Capital Trusts are tax-efficient vehicles aimed at encouraging investment in unquoted companies in the UK. Bear in mind, therefore, that an investment in a Venture Capital Trust carries a higher degree of risk. The tax benefits for a "qualifying subscriber" are 30% income tax relief on the amount invested up to £200,000 along with tax-free income and capital gains after five years.

- Investments under the Enterprise Investment Scheme are also high risk with generous tax benefits.

- Non-resident married couples or civil partners with let property in the United Kingdom should think about putting their properties into joint ownership. It might then be possible for both parties to claim their personal allowance in working out the tax payable on their respective shares of the rental income.

- Foreign nationals, living in the UK, should make the most of their tax favoured non-UK domicile status. The overseas investment income or capital gains of such individuals is not liable to UK taxation unless either the investment income or capital gains are remitted to, or enjoyed in, the UK.

Capital Profits

- Wherever possible try to utilise all your Capital Gains Tax exemption limit each year. Any unused part of the annual limit cannot be carried forward to future years, it is lost.

- By realising gains just after the end of the tax year will delay payment of the tax for 12 months. It may also mean increased taper relief and less tax.

- By splitting sales across the end of a tax year you can make use of your annual exemption limit for two years.

- Husband and wife, as do civil partners, each have their own annual exemption limit. They should consider transferring assets between them, either to use up both exemption limits or to realise gains which would be taxed at a lower rate on one party compared to the other.

- But this does not apply for married couples or civil partners who separate. The opportunity to transfer assets between them free of Capital Gains Tax terminates at the end of the tax year in which separation takes place. The moral here is to separate early on in a tax year to allow sufficient time to divide up valuable assets such as land and shares.

- The excess of your chargeable gains over and above the annual tax-free limit is charged to tax at the rates found by adding the excess to your taxable income. By realising losses to be set against gains you may be able to significantly reduce your Capital Gains Tax liability – particularly if you are a 40% taxpayer.

- You can claim losses for any assets which you own that have become worthless.

- Maybe you have disposed of some assets and are looking at a substantial Capital Gains Tax charge on the profits made? Why not consider reinvesting under the Enterprise Investment Scheme? Only the gain, not the sale proceeds, needs to be reinvested.

- Where it is to your advantage, do not forget to make an election that the gains and losses on disposals of assets which you owned on 31 March 1982 are calculated solely by reference to their market value at that date. The time limit for making this election is two years after the end of the tax year in which the first disposal of an asset you owned on 31 March 1982 takes place.

- When you fill in your Tax Return and work out the taper relief due on your chargeable gains remember the much more generous rate of taper relief which is given on profits on disposals of business assets.

Your Home

- As you do not get tax relief on mortgage interest to buy your own home it might be worthwhile using any spare cash on deposit with a bank or building society to repay some or all of your mortgage.

- If you need more income and do not want to move home, take in a lodger or bed and breakfast guest. Up to £4,250 a year is tax-free under Rent-a-Room relief.

- If you have two or more homes, you are allowed to make an election nominating which one you want to be regarded as your principal private residence for Capital Gains Tax purposes where the profit on sale is free of tax. The election must be made within two years from the date when two or more properties are eligible although it can subsequently be varied.

- The last three years of ownership of a property, which at some point in time has been your only or main residence even by election, are always regarded as though they were lived in by you as the main residence.

- Where a property that has been let has also been occupied as a main residence there is an additional reduction in the taxable gain, relating to the let period, up to a maximum of £40,000.

- Husband and wife or civil partners should consider owning a second home jointly. This could help reduce the Capital Gains Tax payable on a future sale as they may both be able to take advantage of their respective annual exemption limits in working out the tax payable on a profit on sale.

- If your job takes you away from home for up to four years, your period of absence will still count as if you were in occupation of your main residence. The same applies when you work full-time overseas but for an unlimited period.

- It is not uncommon for unmarried couples to each own a home. They may each be able to nominate a main residence for the purposes of Capital Gains Tax.

Retirement

- When in work try to start saving through a pension as soon as you can. You get tax relief on the contributions which, in turn, are invested in a tax-free fund. You can take up to 25% of your fund tax-free.

- As you get near to retirement age for State Pension purposes it is a good idea to get a forecast of what pension you will receive from the DWP. This will also show what additional pension you may be able to purchase by the payment of Class 3 (Voluntary) contributions.

- Maybe it is a good idea to delay taking your State Pension. By the time you receive the lump sum for the deferred pension you might be in a lower tax bracket.

- There are rules allowing elderly couples to transfer the married couples allowance between them. This can sometimes save on tax.

- The income limit for the married couples allowance is by reference to the husband's income or the spouse/civil partner with the higher income as the case may be. These rules apply even if entitlement to this allowance arises because of the others age.

- Elderly couples, in particular, need to give great care and attention to their respective incomes. They should make sure that their investments and savings are arranged such that they do not lose out on the higher personal age and married couples allowances for pensioners in the 65–74 and over 74 age brackets. They should be mindful of the annual income limit above which allowances are restricted. Those couples on modest incomes may be better off tax wise transferring capital between themselves. Alternatively it may pay them to shift some of their savings income into tax-free investments such as National Savings or ISAs. In either case, by doing so, they may avoid losing some of their age related allowances.

- Pensioners with low incomes can "top-up" their income by claiming the Pension Credit.

- Grandparents, or other relatives such as uncles and aunts, can tax-efficiently fund for school fees and other expenses of educating or maintaining grandchildren, nieces or nephews. This might be best done via a Trust, but first of all do take professional advice. The income paid out by the Trustees is the children's income for tax purposes. They should be able to reclaim all or part of the tax suffered by the Trustees on the income distribution by offsetting it against their personal allowance.

Estate Planning

- First and foremost, make a Will and keep it up-to-date. Otherwise your Estate will devolve under the Intestacy Laws and maybe not in a way that you want.

- Always bear in mind that gifts and transfers, during lifetime and on death, between husbands/wives and civil partners are exempt from Inheritance Tax.

- Whenever you can afford to do so, make use of the various exemptions detailed in Chapter 17. By doing so throughout your life you may save on the payment of a significant amount of Inheritance Tax.

- The "normal expenditure out of income" exemption is ideal for dealing with the payment of regular premiums on life policies written in Trust for future generations. As the policy proceeds pass to them free of tax this is, in effect, a substitute for the payment of an Inheritance Tax liability on death which cannot otherwise be avoided.

- Think about rearranging some of your investments so that you can take advantage of the agricultural or business property reliefs. Companies whose shares are quoted on AIM or PLUS and which are trading companies count as unquoted for business property relief purposes.

- Gifts and legacies to charities are exempt from Inheritance Tax. But there are attractive Income Tax and Capital Gains Tax benefits for the donor on lifetime gifts of cash, shares or property to a charity.

- Non-exempt gifts or transfers should be made as early as possible to increase your chances of surviving the seven-year period. Make immediately chargeable gifts – for example transfers into settlement – before those that are potentially exempt.

- Give assets that do not qualify for relief before those that do.

- If possible give assets with low values so that they appreciate in the hands of the recipient and outside of your Estate.

- Consider restricting the chargeable legacies for the next generations to an amount equivalent to the nil rate band for Inheritance Tax, leaving the remainder of your Estate to your spouse or civil partner. He or she can then make gifts and hopefully live for a further seven years.

- Do not waste your nil rate band. It is worth £114,000 (£285,000 at 40%), even if you want to leave your entire Estate to your surviving spouse or partner. Ask your adviser about Discretionary Wills, as you may be able to save some or all of the tax of £114,000.

- In the two years after death, consider the use of a Deed of Variation in order to utilise any available exemptions that would otherwise be lost.

And Finally

- Remember that tax reliefs and rates can change with little or no warning, particularly on a change in Government. So always be ready to react to any changes in legislation.

19 APPENDICES

1 HMRC (Revenue) Explanatory Booklets

No.	*Title*
IR 10	Paying the Right Tax on your Earnings and Pension
IR 14/15	Construction Industry Scheme
IR 20	Residents and Non-Residents – Liability to Tax in the United Kingdom
IR 40	Conditions for getting a Sub-Contractor's Tax Certificate
IR 56	Employed or Self-Employed? A Guide for Tax and National Insurance
IR 64	Giving to Charity by Businesses
IR 65	Giving to Charity by Individuals
IR 111	Bank and Building Society Interest: Are you paying tax when you don't need to?
IR 115	Childcare provided by Employers
IR 116	Guide for Sub-Contractors with Tax Certificates
IR 117	Guide for Sub-Contractors with Registration Cards
IR 138	Living or Retiring Abroad? A guide to UK tax on your UK income and pension
IR 139	Income from Abroad? A guide to UK tax on overseas income
IR 160	HMRC Enquiries under Self-Assessment
IR 170	Blind Person's Allowance
IR 178	Giving Shares and Securities to Charity
SA/BK4	Self-Assessment – A General Guide to Keeping Records
SA/BK8	Self-Assessment – Your Guide
480	Expenses and Benefits: A Tax Guide
CGT 1	Capital Gains Tax: An Introduction
IHT 3	Inheritance Tax: An Introduction
COP 11	Enquiries into Tax Returns by Local Tax Offices
WTC 1	Child Tax Credit and Working Tax Credit: An Introduction
WTC 2	Child Tax Credit and Working Tax Credit: A Guide
WTC 5	Help with the Costs of Childcare: Information for parents and childcare providers

2 Flat-Rate Allowances for Special Clothing and the Upkeep of Tools – 2006/07

(1)	*Fixed rate for all occupations*	£
	Agricultural	70
	Clothing	45
	Forestry	70
	Quarrying	70
	Brass and copper	100
	Precious metals	70
	Textile prints	60
	Food	45
	Glass	60
	Railways (non-crafts people)	70
	Uniformed prison officers	55
	Uniformed bank and building society employees	45
	Uniformed police officers up to and including chief inspector	55
	Uniformed fire fighters and fire officers	60

(2)	*Variable rate depending on category of occupation*	£
	Seamen	130/165
	Iron mining	75/100
	Iron and steel	45/60/120
	Aluminium	45/60/100/130
	Engineering	45/60/100/120
	Shipyards	45/60/75/115
	Vehicles	45/60/105
	Particular engineering	45/60/100/120
	Constructional engineering	45/60/75/115
	Electrical and electricity supply	45/90
	Textiles	60/85
	Leather	45/55
	Printing	30/70/105
	Building materials	45/55/85
	Wood and furniture	45/75/90/115
	Building	45/55/85/105
	Heating	70/90/100
	Public service	45/55
	Healthcare	45/60/70/110

Note   The allowances are only available to manual workers who have to bear the cost of upkeep of tools and special clothing. Other employees, such as office staff, cannot claim them.

3 HMRC (VAT) Notices and Leaflets

No.	Title
700	The VAT Guide
700/1	Should I be Registered for VAT?
700/11	Cancelling your Registration
700/12	Filling in your VAT Return
700/15	The Ins and Outs of VAT
700/18	Relief from VAT on Bad Debts
700/21	Keeping Records and Accounts
700/41	Late Registration Penalty
700/42	Misdeclaration Penalties
700/43	Default Interest
700/45	How to Correct VAT Errors and make Adjustments or Claims
700/50	Default Surcharge
727	Retail Schemes
731	Cash Accounting
732	Annual Accounting
733	Flat Rate Scheme for Small Businesses
930	What if I don't pay?
989	Visits by HMRC Officers
999	Catalogue of Publications
1000	Complaints and Putting Things Right

4 Rates of National Insurance Contributions for 2006/07

CLASS 1 Contributions for Employees

Contributions levied on all weekly earnings above £97.00 but which do not exceed £645.00:

Standard Rate: 11%

Contracted Out: 9.4%

Earnings Threshold	Weekly	£97.00
	Monthly:	£421.00
	Annual:	£5,035.00

Upper Earnings Limit	Weekly:	£645.00
	Monthly:	£2,795.00
	Annual:	£33,540.00

Reduced Rate for Married Women and Widows with a Valid Election Certificate: 4.85%

Contributions levied on all weekly earnings in excess of £645.00: 1%

Rates for Men over 65 and Women over 60: Nil

CLASS 2 Contributions for the Self-Employed

Weekly flat rate: £2.10

Small earnings exception: £4,465.00

CLASS 3 Voluntary Contributions

Weekly rate: £7.55

CLASS 4 Contributions for the Self-Employed

On profits between £5,035 and £33,540: 8%

On profits in excess of £33,540: 1%

5 National Insurance Explanatory Leaflets

No.	Title
CA02	National Insurance Contributions for self employed people with small earnings
CA07	Unpaid and Late-Paid Contributions
CA08	Voluntary National Insurance Contributions
CA09	National Insurance Contributions for Widows or Widowers
CA10	National Insurance Contributions for Divorcees
CA12	Training for Further Employment and Your National Insurance Record
CA13	National Insurance Contributions for Married Women with Reduced Elections
CWL2	National Insurance Contributions for Self-Employed People: Class 2 and Class 4

6 Social Security Benefits

Taxable

Incapacity Benefit after the first 28 weeks (1)
Industrial Death Benefit Pensions
Invalidity Allowance Paid with State Pension
Jobseeker's Allowance
Retirement Pension (1)
Carer's Allowance (1)
Statutory Adoption Pay
Statutory Maternity and Paternity Pay
Statutory Sick Pay
Widowed Parent's Allowance
Bereavement Allowance (1)

Non-taxable

Incapacity Benefit for the first 28 weeks
Income Support
Maternity Allowance
Child Benefit
Child Tax Credit
Child's Special Allowance
Guardian's Allowance
Christmas Bonus for Pensioners
Industrial Injury Benefits
War Disablement Benefits
Disability Living Allowance
Bereavement Payment (Lump Sum)
Earnings Top-Up
Housing Benefit
Jobfinder's Grant
War Pensions
Social Fund Payments
Attendance Allowance
Council Tax Benefit
Redundancy Payment
Vaccine Damage (Lump Sum)
Television Licence Payment
Cold Weather and Winter Fuel Payments
Pension Credit
Working Tax Credit

Note (1) Child dependency additions to these benefits are not taxable.

7 Rates of Main Social Security Benefits for 2006/07

Weekly Rate from 09.04.2006 Onwards
£

Taxable

Retirement pensions

Single person	84.25
Married couple's: both contributors – each	84.25
wife not contributor – addition	50.50
Age addition (over 80) – each	0.25

Bereavement benefits

Bereavement allowance/widow's pension – maximum	84.25
Widowed parent's allowance	84.25

Jobseeker's allowance

Under age 18	34.60
Age 18 to 24	45.50
Age 25 or over	57.45

Incapacity benefit

Long-term	78.50
Increase for age: higher rate	16.50
lower rate	8.25
Short-term (under pension age): lower rate	59.20
higher rate	70.05
(over pension age): lower rate	75.35
higher rate	78.50

Statutory sick pay

Standard rate (weekly earnings threshold £84)	70.05

Statutory maternity, paternity and adoption pay

Rate (weekly earnings threshold £84)	108.85

Non-taxable

Maternity allowance

Standard rate	108.85

Child benefit

Only or eldest child (couple)	17.45
Each other child	11.70
Only or eldest child (lone parent)	17.55

Attendance allowance

Higher rate	62.25
Lower rate	41.65

8   Scope of Liability to Income Tax of Earnings

		Duties of employment performed wholly or partly in the UK		Duties of employment performed wholly outside the UK
		In the UK	Outside the UK	
Foreign emoluments[1]	Employee resident and ordinarily resident in the UK	Liable	Liable	Liable if received in the UK
	Resident but not ordinarily resident	Liable	Liable if received in the UK	Liable if received in the UK
	Not resident	Liable	Not liable	Not liable
Other earnings	Resident and ordinarily resident	Liable	Liable	Liable
	Resident but not ordinarily resident	Liable	Liable if received in the UK	Liable if received in the UK
	Not resident	Liable	Not liable	Not liable

Note   (1) 'Foreign emoluments' is the term to mean the earnings of someone who is not domiciled in the UK and whose employer is not resident in, and is resident outside, the UK.

9 Capital Gains Tax – The Indexation Allowance: April 1998

Starting Months and Years for Indexation

	1982	1983	1984	1985	1986	1987
January	–	0.968	0.872	0.783	0.689	0.626
February	–	0.960	0.865	0.769	0.683	0.620
March	1.047	0.956	0.859	0.752	0.681	0.616
April	1.006	0.929	0.834	0.716	0.665	0.597
May	0.992	0.921	0.828	0.708	0.662	0.596
June	0.987	0.917	0.823	0.704	0.663	0.596
July	0.986	0.906	0.825	0.707	0.667	0.597
August	0.985	0.898	0.808	0.703	0.662	0.593
September	0.987	0.889	0.804	0.704	0.654	0.588
October	0.977	0.883	0.793	0.701	0.652	0.580
November	0.967	0.876	0.788	0.695	0.638	0.573
December	0.971	0.871	0.789	0.693	0.632	0.574

	1988	1989	1990	1991	1992	1993
January	0.574	0.465	0.361	0.249	0.199	0.179
February	0.568	0.454	0.353	0.242	0.193	0.171
March	0.562	0.448	0.339	0.237	0.189	0.167
April	0.537	0.423	0.300	0.222	0.171	0.156
May	0.531	0.414	0.288	0.218	0.167	0.152
June	0.525	0.409	0.283	0.213	0.167	0.153
July	0.524	0.408	0.282	0.215	0.171	0.156
August	0.507	0.404	0.269	0.213	0.171	0.151
September	0.500	0.395	0.258	0.208	0.166	0.146
October	0.485	0.384	0.248	0.204	0.162	0.147
November	0.478	0.372	0.251	0.199	0.164	0.148
December	0.474	0.369	0.252	0.198	0.168	0.146

	1994	1995	1996	1997	1998
January	0.151	0.114	0.083	0.053	0.019
February	0.144	0.107	0.078	0.049	0.014
March	0.141	0.102	0.073	0.046	0.011
April	0.128	0.091	0.066	0.040	–
May	0.124	0.087	0.063	0.036	–
June	0.124	0.085	0.063	0.032	–
July	0.129	0.091	0.067	0.032	–
August	0.124	0.085	0.062	0.026	–
September	0.121	0.080	0.057	0.021	–
October	0.120	0.085	0.057	0.019	–
November	0.119	0.085	0.057	0.019	–
December	0.114	0.079	0.053	0.016	–

10 Main Dates of the Self-Assessment Calendar 6 April 2007 – 5 April 2008

Date	What happens	Who is affected
6 April 2007	2006/07 Tax Returns sent out by HMRC.	Taxpayers who need to fill in an annual Tax Return.
31 July 2007	Second payment on account due for 2006/07.	Those taxpayers who make regular half-yearly payments on account.
	Second £100 penalty levied for failing to submit a 2005/06 Tax Return.	Taxpayers who have not yet completed and sent back their 2005/06 Tax Returns.
	Further automatic 5% surcharge on tax still outstanding for 2005/06.	Late payers of tax still due for 2005/06.
30 September 2007	First filing deadline for completing and returning 2006/07 Tax Returns.	Taxpayers who want HMRC to: • calculate their tax for 2006/07; • collect tax owing for 2006/07 of less than £2,000 through their code number in 2008/09.
31 January 2008	Filing deadline for 2006/07 Tax Returns.	Taxpayers sent a 2006/07 Tax Return.
	Payment date for the balance of tax due for 2006/07 and the first payment on account for 2007/08.	Taxpayers who need to settle either of these liabilities.
1 February 2008	First penalty of £100 charged for the late filing of a 2006/07 Tax Return.	Taxpayers who were sent a 2006/07 Tax Return.
28 February 2008	First automatic 5% surcharge imposed for failing to pay tax due for 2006/07.	Late payers of tax for 2006/07.

20 2007 BUDGET MEASURES

In what will almost certainly be his last Budget, the measures announced by Gordon Brown are aimed at strengthening the Government's economic objective of building a strong economy and a fair society where there is opportunity and security for all. On the personal tax front the main proposals are targeted at modernizing the tax and benefits system, the highlights of which are:

- cutting the basic rate of income tax to 20% from 22%;

- substantially increasing the personal age allowances above indexation;

- increases to both the Child and Working Tax Credits.

All of the measures affecting personal taxes, the payment by employees of National Insurance Contributions, enhanced benefits and tax credits are to be gradually phased in between 2008 and 2011. Full details are given in the section headed 'Looking to the Future'.

Leaving aside the Government's stated aims of these measures, they could also be perceived as a clever strategy designed to help both New Labour's poll ratings and as a grand finale before the curtain falls on Gordon Brown's reign as Chancellor and his anticipated move next door to No.10 Downing Street.

2007/08 Personal Allowances

	£
Personal	
aged under 65	5,225
aged 65–74	7,550
aged 75 and over	7,690
Married couples	
(born before 6 April 1935 and aged less than 75)	*6,285
aged 75 and over	*6,365
minimum amount	*2,440
Income limit for age-related allowances	20,900
Relief for blind person (each)	1,730

* Indicates allowances where tax relief is restricted to 10%.

Tax rates and bands for 2007/08

Band of Taxable Income	Rate of Tax	Tax on Band	Cumulative Tax
£	%	£	£
0–2,230	10	223.00	223.00
2,231–34,600	22	7,121.40	7,344.40
over 34,600	40		

Rates of National Insurance Contributions for 2007/08

CLASS 1 Contributions for Employees

	Standard Rate	Contracted out
Contributions levied on weekly earnings above £100 but which do not exceed £670:	11%	9.4%
If weekly earnings exceed £670:	1%	1%

Reduced Rate for Married Women and Widows with a Valid Election Certificate: 4.85%

If weekly earnings exceed £670: 1%

Men over 65 and Women over 60: Nil

Earnings Threshold	Weekly	£100
	Monthly	£435
	Annually	£5,225
Upper Earnings Limit	Weekly	£670
	Monthly	£2,903
	Annually	£34,840

CLASS 2 Contributions for the Self-Employed

Weekly flat rate: £2.20

Small Earnings Exception: £4,635

CLASS 3 Voluntary Contributions

Weekly rate: £7.80

CLASS 4 Contributions for the Self-Employed

On profits between £5,225 and £34,840: 8%

On profits in excess of £34,840: 1%

Child and Working Tax Credits

The rates for 2007/08 of both the Child and Working Tax Credits are as follows:

Child Tax Credit	£
Family element	545
Family element, baby edition (1st year only)	545
Child element (each child)	1,845
Disabled child element	2,440
Severe disability element	980

Working Tax Credit	£
Basic entitlement	1,730
Additional couples and lone-parent element	1,700
30-hour element	705
Disability element	2,310
Severe disability element	980
50-plus return to work payment, for 16–29 hours	1,185
50-plus return to work payment, for 30-plus hours	1,770

Child care element	
Maximum eligible cost for two or more children	£300 per week
Maximum eligible cost for one child	£175 per week
Percentage of eligible cost covered	80%

For 2007/08 Tax Credits will continue to taper away at a rate of 37% for each £1 of family income over the first income threshold of £5,220 (£14,495 when no Working Tax Credit is claimed).

Company Car Tax

Where a car is made available for an employee's private use there is a tax charge based on the percentage of the list price of the car (subject to a ceiling of £80,000) but graduated according to the level of the car's carbon dioxide (CO_2) emissions. The minimum charge is 15% of list price, increasing to a maximum of 35%.

On and after 6 April 2008 there will be a 2% discount from the appropriate percentage rate for cars manufactured to run on E85 fuel.

Landlords' energy saving allowance

From 6 April 2007 expenditure on floor insulation has been added to the list of deductions you can claim against your rental income. Furthermore, the expenditure limit of £1,500 is now available for each property, rather than for each building. This allowance will be available until 2015.

Capital allowances

The 50% first year allowance for spending by small businesses on information and communications technology or for expenditure on plant, machinery, fixtures and fittings, but not motor cars, is extended for a further 12 months until 5 April 2008.

Homes owned abroad through a company

Ownership of an overseas property is increasingly widespread and for many innocent reasons it is common to own such property via a company. Those connected with the company may find themselves taxable on a benefit in kind in respect to their use of the property. The Government intend to introduce retrospective legislation exempting such benefits in kind where the overseas property is owned by a company that is in turn owned by individuals whose sole activity is holding that property for occupation.

Value Added Tax

The Value Added Tax registration threshold is increased with effect from 1 April 2007 from annual taxable turnover of £61,000 to £64,000. The cancellation of registration limit goes up from £59,000 to £62,000.

The fuel scale charge rules allow businesses to use an average private fuel charge for each car, thereby reducing the administration required to calculate the exact split between reclaimable business fuel and non-reclaimable private fuel. For accounting periods beginning on or after 1 May 2007, the fuel scale charge will be based on carbon dioxide emissions, similar to that used for the company car benefit in kind charge.

Capital Gains Tax

The Capital Gains Tax annual exemption limit is increased to £9,200 for 2007/08.

Inheritance tax

From 6 April 2007 the nil rate band increases from £285,000 to £300,000, with further staged increases to £325,000 and £350,000 by April 2009 and 2010 respectively.

Tax compliance

A single penalty regime is being introduced for incorrect returns covering all aspects of the tax system. This will replace the separate regimes currently in force and the informal method of mitigating these penalties based on the behaviour and co-operation of the taxpayer. There will be:

- no penalty where a taxpayer makes a mistake;

- moderate penalties for failures to take reasonable care;

- higher penalties for deliberate action; and

- still higher penalties for deliberate action with concealment.

Guidance on the operation of the new regime is also promised.

In what appears to be an attempt to encourage taxpayers to file their Tax Returns earlier, the period during which the Revenue can enquire into a Tax Return will close one year after its submission. For personal Tax Returns this will first of all apply for 2007/08 Returns.

Furthermore, the filing deadline for personal Tax Returns for 2007/08 and later years submitted in paper form will be 31 October after the end of the tax year. For Tax Returns filed online, the deadline will remain at the following 31 January.

Looking to the Future

Many of the measures announced by the Chancellor will not take effect immediately, namely:

Measure	*Date of introduction*
• The basic rate of income tax will come down from 22% to 20%.	2008/09
• In the same year the 10% starting rate will be removed for earned income and pensions. But it will still be available for savings income and capital gains.	2008/09
• The personal allowances for those in the 65–74 and over 74 age brackets will be increased by £1,180 over and above indexation.	April 2008
• The personal allowance for an individual aged 75 and over will be £10,000.	2011/12
• Increasing the upper earnings limit for national insurance by £75 a week above indexation.	April 2008
• Fully aligning the upper earnings limit for national insurance with the higher rate tax threshold.	April 2009
• Raising the aligned upper earnings limit for national insurance and higher rate tax threshold by £800 more than indexation.	April 2009
• On Tax Credits	
– increasing the child element of the Child Tax Credit by £150 a year above earnings indexation.	April 2008
– raising the threshold for Working Tax Credit by £1,200.	April 2008
– raising the withdrawal rate for Tax Credits by 2% to 39%.	April 2008
• Increasing the weekly rate of Child Benefit for the eldest child to £20.	April 2010

- Raising the limit for investments in an Individual Savings Account to £7,200 with an increase in the cash limit to £3,600.   April 2008
- Subject to further consultation a new Annual Investment Allowance for the first £50,000 spent on plant and machinery will replace the first year allowances for small and medium sized businesses.   2008/09
- The rate of writing down allowances for capital allowances purposes on the general pool of expenditure will be reduced from 25% to 20%.   2008/09